HOPE IN ISOLATION

90-DAY DEVOTIONAL

REBECCA CARPENTER

deepwatersbooks.com

Hope in Isolation: 90-Day Devotional

Copyright © 2022 Rebecca Carpenter

Published by Deep Waters Books, P.O. Box 692301, Orlando, FL 32869
www.deepwatersbooks.com

Cover Photo Credit: Rebecca Carpenter

Cover Design: Doni Keene

KEENE IDEAS CREATIVE, 11931 Elbert Street, Clermont, FL 34711

First Printing 2022

Printed in the United States of America

All Scripture quotations, unless otherwise indicated, are taken from the Holy Bible, New International Version®, NIV®. Copyright ©1973, 1978, 1984, 2011 by Biblica, Inc.™ Used by permission of Zondervan. All rights reserved worldwide. www.zondervan.com. The "NIV" and "New International Version" are trademarks registered in the United States Patent and Trademark Office by Biblica, Inc.™

Scripture quotations marked NKJV are taken from the New King James Version®. Copyright © 1982 by Thomas Nelson. Used by permission. All rights reserved.

Scripture quotations marked VOICE are taken from The Voice™. Copyright © 2012 by Ecclesia Bible Society. Used by permission. All rights reserved.

Identifiers: ISBN: (Hardcover) 978-1-956520-09-5 | ISBN: (Paperback) 978-1-956520-08-8 | LCCN: 2022913489

Publisher's Cataloging-in-Publication data
Names: Carpenter, Rebecca, author.
Title: Hope in isolation / Rebecca Carpenter
Description: Orlando, FL: Deep Waters Books, 2022.
Identifiers: LCCN: 2022913489 | ISBN: 978-1-956520-08-8 (paperback) | 978-1-956520-09-5 (hardcover)
Subjects: LCSH Christianity--Prayers and devotions. | Grief--Religious aspects--Christianity. | Prayers. | Spiritual life--Christianity. | Christian life. | BISAC RELIGION / Christian Living / Devotional | RELIGION / Christian Living / Death, Grief, Bereavement
Classification: LCC BV245 .C37 2022 | DDC 242/.8--dc23

PRAISE FOR REBECCA CARPENTER

"Rebecca Carpenter's latest book, *Hope in Isolation*, is filled with encouraging and healing words of hope from one who has known the grief of losing a spouse followed by an extended time of seclusion during the pandemic. Isolation does not respond well to quick fixes or instant healing. It is an extended journey that needs continued encouragement from those who can walk with us. Rebecca's ninety-day devotional is designed as a daily journey to reflect on God's promises of hope, which touches the mind through the heart. This is a much-needed and helpful resource for those walking through a sense of loneliness and for those who are caregivers for others."

> The Reverend Dr. Larry Selig
> Retired Pastor, Mt. Lebanon United Presbyterian Church,
> Pittsburgh, PA
> Author, *5 Prayers God Loves to Answer*

"Through these long and uncertain days of a global pandemic, Rebecca invites us to dig deeper in God's Word and to go outside to observe God's handiwork. With a keen eye and an open heart, she offers us a way to persevere and live with hope in these troubled times. Her reflections will inspire you to awaken your senses to God's presence and promises."

> John Tardonia
> Pastor, Northland Church, Orlando, FL

"Rebecca Carpenter's *Hope in Isolation* is a guide for anyone experiencing the darkness of solitude, whether due to a pandemic or for any other reason. In our current world, where so many are feeling lost and forlorn, Rebecca's optimism and faith are infectious! This is a real 'feel good' book."

Maura McKay
Retired VP of Operations, Harland Financial Solutions

"Rebecca's book has changed my life! These devotionals are powerful! Each one is overflowing with wisdom, love, encouragement, and hope. Her stories combined with the supporting verses and prayers remind me of God's infinite love for us. Rebecca's writing style is relatable, candid, and honest, and her love for God and the reader are deeply felt with each page. After reading her devotionals, I'm left with a profound sense of calmness and joy. Her stories are beautifully narrated; the descriptions are so well expressed that they place the reader in the midst of God's presence."

Gretchka Saliceti
Aspiring Author & Yoga Instructor

"Even though I have walked through and experienced most of these stories firsthand with my beloved grandma, each time I read her writings, I am refreshed by her faith in God. The Lord has given her a gift of writing to turn our hearts filled with despair and fear to ones of hope, joy, and peace. Even in hard times, such as COVID, God's grace and glory shine through!"

Emily Storms
Granddaughter and High School Student
Author, "Sisterhood" Blog

"Rebecca Carpenter's *Hope in Isolation* comforts readers who feel lonely and isolated due to the coronavirus pandemic or other various causes. Through each one of her ninety timely devotional writings, she leads us through these turbulent times. Each message combats the media's dire messages of sickness, death, and despair with powerful encouragements to look to God for our hope, peace, and purpose. Ms. Carpenter shares her intimate personal experiences of isolation to help us cope with the monotonous din in our own lives. Her artful writings help us overcome oppression and despair no matter the cause, and lead us on a path of growing faith, transformation, and gratitude for our many blessings. She reassures us that while we may feel isolated and lonely, we never walk alone when we cling to the hand of God."

Jeanne LeMay
Author, *Dear God I'm Desperate: Women Have Issues, God Has Answers*

CONTENTS

1. Day 1: Looking Ahead to the Goal — 1
2. Day 2: Isolation During Sickness — 3
3. Day 3: Released Captive — 5
4. Day 4: Creation Overcomes Chaos — 7
5. Day 5: Hoarding Treasures — 9
6. Day 6: Holding Tight — 11
7. Day 7: Joyful Trees — 13
8. Day 8: From Buds to Blooms — 15
9. Day 9: Emergence of Spring — 17
10. Day 10: Treasures Around Me — 19
11. Day 11: Glimmers of Hope — 21
12. Day 12: Faith in an Ebony Sky — 23
13. Day 13: Fatigue But Not Death — 25
14. Day 14: Weeks of Quarantine — 27
15. Day 15: Is It True? Is It Kind? Is It Helpful? — 29
16. Day 16: Palm Sunday's Latest Oppression — 31
17. Day 17: Mailbox Fronds — 33
18. Day 18: Tears of Sorrow — 35
19. Day 19: Darkness and Despair — 37
20. Day 20: Mournful Waiting — 39
21. Day 21: The Final Easter Picture — 41
22. Day 22: A Novel Easter Sunrise — 43
23. Day 23: Wondrous Easter at Home — 45
24. Day 24: Monarch Miracles — 47
25. Day 25: Conflicting Alerts — 49
26. Day 26: Where Is Your Focus? — 51
27. Day 27: God's Astounding Gifts — 53
28. Day 28: Missing Another Miracle — 55
29. Day 29: Chrysalis of Life — 57
30. Day 30: Contentment During the Storms — 59
31. Day 31: Trusting God for Mother's Day — 61
32. Day 32: Blessing in Community — 63
33. Day 33: Returning to My Pink Bike — 65

34. Day 34: Pressing Toward the Goal — 67
35. Day 35: Finding Joy and Purpose — 69
36. Day 36: Waiting on My Bread — 71
37. Day 37: Released from My Cage — 73
38. Day 38: An Altered Adventure — 75
39. Day 39: Small But Powerful — 77
40. Day 40: An Unseen World — 79
41. Day 41: Limp and Lifeless — 81
42. Day 42: Lessons from Solitude — 83
43. Day 43: Bible Study Party — 85
44. Day 44: Destructive Weeds — 87
45. Day 45: Predicted or Unpredicted Storms — 89
46. Day 46: A Sparkle in the Mess — 91
47. Day 47: Hummingbirds, Bees, and Butterflies — 93
48. Day 48: Toppled Bush — 95
49. Day 49: Mountains We Climb — 97
50. Day 50: Time at the Lab — 99
51. Day 51: Visiting Cardinals — 101
52. Day 52: Creatures in the Dark — 103
53. Day 53: Kindness at Walmart — 105
54. Day 54: Turbulent Times — 107
55. Day 55: Danger Beneath the Surface — 109
56. Day 56: Stabs of Pain — 111
57. Day 57: A Thanksgiving in Solitude — 113
58. Day 58: An Alphabet of Thankfulness — 115
59. Day 59: The Pink Gift — 117
60. Day 60: Play Like Children — 119
61. Day 61: Where Is Baby Jesus? — 121
62. Day 62: No Room — 123
63. Day 63: Heavenly Messengers — 125
64. Day 64: The Christmas Star — 127
65. Day 65: Life in Despair — 129
66. Day 66: Warning — 131
67. Day 67: A New Year — 133
68. Day 68: Empty Shelves and Lives — 135
69. Day 69: Flickering Flames — 137
70. Day 70: Peeling Shoes — 139
71. Day 71: Out-of-Season Butterflies — 141

72.	Day 72: Starkness of a Winter Day	143
73.	Day 73: A Nostalgic Pinwheel	145
74.	Day 74: Neglected Plants	147
75.	Day 75: From Fog to Sunshine	149
76.	Day 76: Standing Strong in the Storms	151
77.	Day 77: A Bright Spot in the Gloom	153
78.	Day 78: Unappreciated Thumbs	155
79.	Day 79: Another Day of Bleakness?	157
80.	Day 80: A Stubborn Attitude	159
81.	Day 81: Me, Selfish?	161
82.	Day 82: Cloaked with Peace	163
83.	Day 83: Shattered Pieces	165
84.	Day 84: The Massive Spider Web	167
85.	Day 85: Not COVID!	169
86.	Day 86: Don't Take Away Blessings	171
87.	Day 87: The Yellow Mums	173
88.	Day 88: Unclean—Stay Away!	175
89.	Day 89: The Retreat in New Hampshire	177
90.	Day 90: The Diverse Eleven	179
91.	Bonus Day 91: The Lost Suitcase	181
	Author Bio	184
	Also by Rebecca Carpenter	185
	Deep Waters Books	186

NOTE FROM THE AUTHOR

Dear Reader,
My times of isolation didn't start with hope. As a young mother with two children to raise after an unwanted divorce, I felt rejected. Profound feelings of loneliness came with my new solitude.
Years later, losing my parents and new husband made me an orphan and a widow within a few months. I couldn't even say those words for a long time. Grief hit me and brought a season of more intense separation.
The pandemic and the effects of quarantine magnified the already-painful isolation of living alone.
Despite traveling through the valley of the shadow of death, I learned to trust God, accept Jesus more fully, and listen to the Holy Spirit.
It was only then that I truly experienced hope.
I pray that these devotionals give you hope as well.
In Christ alone,
Rebecca Carpenter

DAY 1: LOOKING AHEAD TO THE GOAL

Forgetting what is behind and straining toward what is ahead, I press on toward the goal to win the prize for which God has called me heavenward in Christ Jesus....
But our citizenship is in heaven. And we eagerly await a savior from there, the Lord Jesus Christ, who, by the power that enables him to bring everything under his control, will transform our lowly bodies so that they will be like his glorious body.
~ Philippians 3:13–14, 20–21

Sunlight beamed through the trees across the lake like gigantic headlights on a dark night. Water droplets beat out a steady rhythm on the downspout. An occasional chirp drifted through the hushed dawn.

When the sun crawled out of bed, the lake wrinkled like a mussed comforter. Birds awoke. A blue heron circled my yard and landed on the shore. Warbling birds joined together in a delightful chorus. A pair of ducks swam lazily. Gray cloud curtains pushed back to reveal a clear blue sky.

Just as the dark night transformed into a bright, cheerful morning, I received faith for an easier, more normal year. I found my heart turning from its laments over the painful past toward anticipation of the opportunities that lay ahead.

Spending time with God in my special retreat offers me encouragement and comfort. When I read of his faithfulness, love, and protection, I am reminded of how he has provided for me and countless others for centuries. When I leave my serene spot, I return to the chaos of the world, but not without hope.

This week brought news of the death of a friend's brother, a recent widower in deep grief over the passing of his wife, a friend devastated by the recent loss of her husband, a gravely ill cousin, and a widow's injury from a fall. Each time I learned of loss or sorrow, my heart ached. Because of my own pain, I understood and wanted to offer comfort as I had been consoled.

I never planned nor wanted a ministry to the grieving, but that is what I have been given. Over and over, God has placed hurting people in my life.

At first, I resisted because I thought their misery would reignite my own. Sometimes it does. However, I have learned to embrace people in their sorrows while God refines and teaches me. I am thankful when I make even a small difference in someone else's life.

As this new year began, I looked forward to what God had prepared for me. I don't want to live in the difficult past or imagine horrible circumstances in the future. Since this is not our home, help us, God, to live each day fully with Jesus.

Father, as we begin a new year and each new season, help us press on toward our goal for the prize as we journey to heaven. This is not our home, so we can look ahead to heaven where there will be no more tears or sadness.
Amen.

DAY 2: ISOLATION DURING SICKNESS

When sickness comes, the Eternal is beside them—
to comfort them on their sickbeds and restore them to health.
~ Psalm 41:3 VOICE

Coughing. Sniffling. Weariness. For days, I shuffled from my bed to the couch and wrapped myself in a warm, fuzzy blanket. With much effort, I occasionally ventured to the kitchen for a drink. For days, I only walked outside to get mail or take out the garbage. Thankfully, a kind neighbor returned the trash can to my garage door.

I prayed continually that my health would improve. When that didn't happen right away, plans had to be canceled. I missed my Bible study, my granddaughter's softball game, an Amy Grant concert, and a friend's birthday lunch. I couldn't volunteer at the library bookstore or at church, as I usually did.

Normal activities stopped completely for me while the rest of the world lived normally. Being in seclusion made me feel sorry for myself.

Then my doorbell rang. A friend handed me throat lozenges. A few hours later, another neighbor brought a large container of chicken noodle soup. Their kindnesses blew away my sadness.

During this bout with bronchitis, my phone pinged with text messages from family and friends asking how I was doing. They offered to help out and assured me they were praying, which helped relieve my loneliness.

Even though I regretted missing so much and spent day after day alone, God provided a long list of people to love and serve me. My illness disabled me for a time but wasn't terminal.

I rested in my comfortable home and drank healthy fluids to stay hydrated. Prepared meals from my freezer, along with a supply from neighbors, kept me well fed. My doctor gave me a checkup and medication.

Millions of people around the world have little access to clean water, sufficient food, safe housing, or adequate medical care. Many find themselves alone and discouraged, with little hope. How fortunate I am to be loved and cared for.

Even in isolation, God provides.

Loving Father, thank you for nursing us when we are sick and in pain. Bless those who struggle and feel hopeless.
Amen.

DAY 3: RELEASED CAPTIVE

*And we know that in all things God works for the
good of those who love him, who have been
called according to his purpose.*
~ Romans 8:28

Faint wisps of white clouds stretched across the brilliant blue sky. Birdsong accompanied the artistic display. Like a released captive, I enjoyed my morning walk with a sense of freedom. Two weeks of nasty bronchitis and fatigue had isolated me from the world.

Bursts of color painted the entire neighborhood. Pink and white azaleas announced spring as they waltzed in the breeze. Cream and red amaryllises waved their faces. Purple, pink, and yellow mums dotted landscapes. Every flower made my heart smile.

Just above the trees, a formation of three single-engine planes hummed as they flew over the homes. Later, a fourth plane merged into the formation. A parade of neighbors walked and rode bikes past me. We greeted each other with a smile and hello.

After being inside for days and days, everything around me seemed new and exciting.

Despite the horrific news reports and catastrophes around the world, neighbors escaped to the beauty of a spring morning. God's creation reminded me to appreciate everything around me, both small and large.

Later in the day, as I turned my car onto the interstate, I thanked God for my health and the ability to leave my home. I praised him for everything I saw on my forty-minute trip to my son's home.

When I arrived, my spunky ten-year-old granddaughter, Molly, opened the door and hugged me. Her embrace surrounded me with love. How I had missed her smile, laughter, and enthusiasm while cooped up.

The aroma of homemade banana bread filled their home. My daughter-in-law Anne smiled as I walked into the kitchen. What a gift to see her on her feet again after she had been sick.

My granddaughter Ashlyn and I went shopping and then out to lunch. We giggled and ate, loving the opportunity to finally be together again.

My thankfulness swelled after being sick and confined.

Sometimes God puts us in uncomfortable situations to make us appreciate all that we have.

Loving Father, we don't see the benefits of difficult situations as we go through them. Thank you for being patient with us as you see the whole picture and weave the blessings and trials together into something beautiful.
Amen.

DAY 4: CREATION OVERCOMES CHAOS

For the Spirit God gave us does not make us timid, but gives us power, love and self-discipline.
~ 2 Timothy 1:7

Like a burst of flames, sunrise lit up the sky beyond the lake. A new day of opportunities awaited me.

Endless days of dire predictions and depressing charts depicting the increasing numbers of those infected and dying from the coronavirus filled my mind. Schools, churches, businesses, and even Disney were closed.

Officials warned of the horrible consequences of contracting the virus, and guidelines for citizens to follow circulated in the media. After all the terrible news, newscasters and doctors said to remain calm. But anyone who constantly watches and listens to the alarming newscasts becomes fearful and anxious.

Thankfully, the beautiful morning reminded me that the sun comes up every day. God doesn't shut down his creation. Birds continue to sing joyously. Flowers bloom in vibrant colors. New leaves sprout from dormant branches even with the world in turmoil.

In the chaos, I realized that we are not in control. Of course, as a society, we tried to contain the illness and follow the safety guidelines, but there was no guarantee against getting sick. Reality hit—only God controls this world.

I prayed, and the Lord revealed to me those who are frightened and need prayer. After making a few phone calls, and sending out emails and text messages full of Scripture passages and words of hope, I felt lighter and more at peace.

Isolation from normal activities offers opportunities to fully engage with family and friends whether near or far away. In the stillness, I found myself more alert during my walks and truly appreciated the trees, flowers, and wildlife, like the sandhill cranes walking in my path.

I made a choice to be productive. I tackled a pile of books I wanted to read and started painting pictures of God's creation. With a renewed sense of purpose, I cleaned out my closets, wrote letters to loved ones, and accomplished neglected chores (my baseboards never looked so good). Funny sitcoms, stand-up comics, and hysterical movies played on my television. Shocked by the endless possibilities surrounding me, I praised God for my new sense of time freedom.

Instead of complaining about what I lost during the lockdown and drafting horrendous stories in my head, I focused on the present and became thankful for all my blessings.

Just as panic spreads quickly, so can love, kindness, and calmness.

Loving Father, in our distress and fears, give us power and love as we face unwelcome circumstances.
Amen.

DAY 5: HOARDING TREASURES

*"Do not lay up for yourselves treasures on earth,
where moth and rust destroy and where thieves break
in and steal; but lay up for yourselves treasures in
heaven, where neither moth nor rust destroys and
where thieves do not break in and steal. For where
your treasure is, there your heart will be also."*
~ Matthew 6:19–21 NKJV

These verses from the book of Matthew brought thoughts of toilet paper and hand sanitizer. People hoarded those items. They selfishly grabbed milk and eggs even when they had plenty at home. Some houses must have overflowed with excess supplies while others had none. Because of fear and anxiety, people tried to gain control of something in their lives. Desperate, frightened people react in bizarre ways.

Since my faith is in Jesus and not toilet paper, I had peace as absurdity swirled around me. An assurance that God is in control, and not the authorities, bestows peace on God's children.

My heart broke for the illnesses and deaths around the world. My prayers centered on bringing an end to the pandemic and the restoration of peace.

Even in isolation, God cares and has work for us to do. Our church leadership told us to pray, connect, serve, and give. We can pray and give from home easily. However, it takes some creativity to know how to connect and serve when required to stay secluded.

Thankfully, emails, text messages, Zoom calls, letters, and actual phone calls kept people connected. Friends met for backyard picnics. Neighbors picked up grocery items for others when they went shopping, so everyone didn't have to leave home. Folks checked on those who lived alone. Notes and devotionals left at neighbors' doors reminded them that someone cared.

God's Word kept me connected to him and gave me peace and serenity even in turbulent times.

God, you are our only hope. Give us peace and contentment
when nothing around us is peaceful.
Amen.

DAY 6: HOLDING TIGHT

*He gives strength to the weary and increases the power of the weak.
Even youths grow tired and weary, and young men stumble and
fall; but those who hope in the Lord will renew their strength.
They will soar on wings like eagles; they will run and not grow
weary, they will walk and not be faint.*
~ *Isaiah 40:29–31*

At the peak of a bare cypress tree, a great white egret pulled his body into a small ball. He clung tightly to the skinny top branch and scanned the lake. His slender neck formed an "S" shape as his eyes shifted back and forth. Without swaying, his spindly legs held him firmly.

I stared in amazement at his inspiring feat. Behind him, a blanket of gray swathed the pink sunrise. Despite the swiftly gathering gloom around him, the egret remained stoic and focused.

His calmness in a precarious position contrasted with the anxiety and fear spreading around the world. Contradicting facts and opinions screamed from the television and on social media. Overwhelming uncertainty caused panic.

Like the majestic bird, I pause each morning in my serene, lakeside retreat. I cling to God by reading and meditating on his Word. Daily devotionals give me insight. Praying helps me focus and guides me for the day.

Delighting in God's creation brings me closer to him too. Watching wildlife slows me down and reminds me how blessed I am. Stunning flowers, unique animals, and awesome sunrises deliver joy. Animals teach lessons of survival, focus, and doing what they were created to do in their environments.

For a few minutes, the compressed white bird rested and prepared for whatever he needed to do next. At just the right time, he lifted his vast wings, took flight, and confidently soared into the unknown.

As disturbing news and alarming predictions try to overtake logic, I have a renewed sense of the importance of retreating and holding tightly to God as he provides peace and strength for the journey ahead.

Loving Father, in our unsettled world, you are
constantly with us as we are sheltered under your
wings. Give us joy for the days ahead.
Amen.

DAY 7: JOYFUL TREES

You will go out in joy and be led forth in peace;
the mountains and hills will burst into song before
you, and all the trees of the field will clap their hands.
~ Isaiah 55:12

During my time of solitude, spring arrived. A group of seven cypress trees on the shoreline by my home began a transformation that I watched each day.

At first, naked and uneven limbs revealed knotty scars, misshapen branches, and tilted trunks. Day by day, changes came as the weather warmed. Like sheltering parents, the two end trees sprouted first with barely noticeable tufts of green. Gradually, bright emerald needles developed and swathed every tree in the group like a lovely scarf.

Needles blocked a clear view of the lake, but I watched birds perch and squirrels scuttle before they hid in the fresh foliage for safety. On rainy days, water clung to and weighed down branches. Strong breezes shook off moisture like a dog after its bath. When storms hit, the wind whipped limbs back and forth. After dawn, sunlight sparkled on dew-drenched needles.

Each day brought changes to the developing trees. I delighted to see growth and more wildlife. The small grove gave me peace and contentment in a troubled time.

A few years ago when a hurricane hit our area, two of the trees started to lean toward the lake. Thankfully, they didn't topple; their strong roots holding them upright. Despite all kinds of weather, they continued growing in their new, slanted directions.

When storms of life hit, we have choices. We can either bend and bounce back or fall down in defeat. Imagine the testimony of our faith to others if we remain steadfast in the altered direction, adapting and flourishing with God as our stronghold.

Father, we can find joy and peace as we experience the
beauty and resilience of nature.
Show us the direction
we must go.
Amen.

DAY 8: FROM BUDS TO BLOOMS

But the plans of the L<small>ORD</small> stand firm forever,
the purposes of his heart
through all generations.
~ Psalm 33:11

African irises clustered at the edge of my patio. Blades of green waved in the wind. Three white buds topped slender stems. When we moved from the house Alan and I built several years ago, we brought clumps of the irises and transplanted them around our new home.

I concentrated on reading the Bible and my daily devotionals for a while. When I glanced at the flowers, a full bloom surprised me. Half an hour later, the second bud burst into a delicate blossom. A third bud was close to opening too. Even though the floras unfurled only a few feet away from me, I missed the transformation.

I stared intently at the last bud, hoping to watch it unfold. A parade of ducks in my yard diverted my attention for a few seconds. During that brief period, the final iris expanded. I sighed, having failed to see any of them unfurl.

My attention returned to the ducks as they waddled to the lake. In a perfect "V" formation, they swam from the shore to the middle of the lake with a wake flowing behind them. Unseen webbed feet propelled them across the once-placid water.

Looking at my newly exposed flowers and the swimming ducks, I thought of how God often works in ways I don't notice. I am able to observe only parts of the plan, but he sees the whole picture.

As we lived in a pandemic state-of-isolation, grave predictions for the economy, our health, and foreign relations infiltrated the news media. Fear and anguish abounded, but God was not surprised by the widespread catastrophe. He continued to work in miraculous ways behind the scenes. If we trust in him, we will have peace and, eventually, see the results of his plan.

Father, in uncertain times, replace fear with your peace.
Remind us that you are working even when we don't see it.
Help us trust in you.
Amen.

DAY 9: EMERGENCE OF SPRING

*I waited patiently for the LORD; he turned to me and heard my cry.
He lifted me out of the slimy pit, out of the mud and mire; he set
my feet on a rock and gave me a firm place to stand. He put a new
song in my mouth, a hymn of praise to our God. Many will see and
fear the LORD and put their trust in him.*
~ Psalm 40:1–4

During the winter, needles dropped from the line of seven cypress trees near my home along the lake. Then the weather warmed, but the middle five remained barren and gloomy.

Surprisingly, bright green shoots burst open almost overnight on the two trees at each end. Feathery green wisps clothed them like chiffon. When sunlight reached their branches, the dew-drenched needles sparkled. Their vibrant beauty gave hope that the other trees would soon be revived.

The emergence of spring produced a sense of optimism in my heart that our communities, our country, and the world would also emerge from the effects of the pandemic. It reminded me that just as my trees flourish and rebound from harsh conditions, so will we.

Of course, concerns and uncertainties will always remain. But as we work together, support one another, and pray, we can come out of any disaster stronger and wiser.

We don't control the world, but we can control our reactions. Even in difficult times, we can be thankful and reach out to those around us.

Heavenly Father, protect us in our times of trouble and give us hope for the future. Help us trust and praise you in every season.
Amen.

DAY 10: TREASURES AROUND ME

This is the day the LORD has made;
We will rejoice and be glad in it.
~ Psalm 118:24 NKJV

From my chair on the patio, I quietly listened to a symphony of delightful bird melodies. Reflections of colorful trees on the lake held my attention as I studied each one. Spring brought the transformation of cypress trees from bare limbs to full foliage. Within the beauty, I also noticed dangling branches that needed to be trimmed.

A profusion of vibrant, colorful flowers decorated my yard. Each species was a distinct color and unique design. Pots of peppermint and basil, waiting to be picked, grew in large planters on my patio.

Bumblebees, butterflies, and hummingbirds flitted around my flower garden. The bees and butterflies visited flowers of every color, while the hummingbirds bypassed pink, purple, and white blooms to sip only from orange ones.

As I studied the flora and fauna close to me, I noticed a deer across the lake. She walked alone instead of with companions who used to visit with her. Later, a black bear emerged from the forest not far from where the deer first appeared. He ambled along the shore and disappeared into the brush at the end of the lake. Although he was a frequent visitor to the neighborhood, this was my first bear sighting at this home.

Each time I sit on my patio and relax, God's peace wraps me like a warm blanket. A treasure awaits daily when I take time to observe and treasure the gifts of nature around me. In my little sanctuary, God faithfully shows up and floods me with gratitude.

Each morning before I get out of bed, I repeat Psalm 118:24: "This is the day the Lord has made; We will rejoice and be glad in it." That verse helps me focus on what's important each day, despite the uncertainty surrounding me.

Thankfully, we can rejoice and appreciate God's creation around us.

Loving Father, we rejoice each day for the treasures you have given us in your creation.
Amen.

DAY 11: GLIMMERS OF HOPE

Trust in the Lord with all your heart and lean not on your own understanding; in all your ways submit to him, and he will make your paths straight. Do not be wise in your own eyes; fear the Lord and shun evil.
~ Proverbs 3:5–7

A cloak of black wrapped the sky. Twinkling stars and bright planets created a wondrous display. A slice of the moon, the largest and brightest object in the inky expanse, glowed through a gap between trees. A chorus of crickets droned before dawn. Traffic hummed on a highway outside my community.

Since I enjoy sunrises and the dawn's awakening, I normally stay inside until the sun peaks over the horizon. But darkness seemed more fitting during my period of isolation. Beyond the patio light, I saw stars, planets, and a sliver of the moon.

Blackness concealed bears, armadillos, coyotes, eagles, cranes, turkeys, and other wildlife that had been spotted in my neighborhood. They could have been waiting in my yard just beyond my patio—ready to pounce, rip, or attack.

During the day, I enjoy watching the birds, deer, turtles, butterflies, and other creatures. However, in the darkness, fearful thoughts concoct potential dangers lurking outside my screen.

In the uncertainty of the pandemic, our minds formed all sorts of horrible scenarios. What-ifs produced sleepless nights. Anxiety and distress replaced peace and reason.

As the sky turned from an inky black to pale blue, birds awoke and sang a cheery welcome to the day.

Just as the sun appears each day, we eventually emerge out of our trials. Glimmers of hope gradually emerge from our isolation, chaos, and turbulence.

Daily, we can choose how to respond to difficulties. Every morning, no matter how I feel, I spend time reading the Bible, praying, and delighting in the beauty of God's creation.

Instead of constantly watching stories of doom on the news, I fill myself with uplifting and positive shows and books. I drop off flowers to widows and leave cards for the lonely.

I find myself embracing the wisdom, hope, and encouragement in the Psalms and Proverbs, instead of the imagined stories of destruction.

Loving Father, as we navigate through uncertain
times, hold us in your arms and show us your way.
Give us hope despite the despair found in the world.
Amen.

DAY 12: FAITH IN AN EBONY SKY

*Then God said, "Let there be lights in the firmament of the heavens
to divide the day from the night; and let them be for signs
and seasons, and for days and years; and let there be for lights in
the firmament of the heavens to give light on the earth"; and it was
so. Then God made two great lights: the greater light to rule the
day, and the lesser light to rule the night. He made the stars
also. God set them in the firmament of the heavens to give light on
the earth, and to rule over the day and over the night, and to divide
the light from the darkness. And God saw that it was good.*
~ Genesis 1:14–18 NKJV

Outside my porch, I gazed at the twinkling stars scattered across an ebony sky. A planet gleamed brighter and larger than the countless sparkling stars. A crescent moon hung just above the shadowy trees.

I marveled at the orderliness of the universe around me, with every celestial body positioned in perfect harmony. Man didn't place Earth in an exact orbit around the sun so that life would be sustained. Unseen gravity keeps the stars, planets, and even us from flying off into space. The enormity of the universe with its countless galaxies is beyond my comprehension. I have no idea how it all works together, but God does.

As wonder filled my mind, the darkness of night ebbed. A brief pink sunrise blushed and vanished quickly within a covering of clouds.

Faith reassures me that the predawn scene will once again return. As our world rotates, the predictable universe remains around us. When darkness returns, I will again see the stars, planets, and our moon.

From the magnitude of space to microscopic viruses, God creates, understands, and comforts us. He is in control. And because he has been faithful in other things, I must remember that he controls everything, including earthly calamities and planetary cataclysms. Jesus's guidance and peace give us the confidence to have hope at all times, despite what is swirling around us.

Creator of the universe, when we see the magnitude of the stars and planets, we see your awesomeness and power. If you can create the Milky Way, then we can depend on you to take care of us at all times. Heal those who are sick, and cure our land.
Amen.

DAY 13: FATIGUE BUT NOT DEATH

Do you not know? Have you not heard?
*The L*ORD *is the everlasting God,*
the Creator of the ends of the earth.
He will not grow tired or weary, and
his understanding no one can fathom.
He gives strength to the weary and increases the power of the
weak. Even youths grow tired and weary, and young men stumble
*and fall; but those who hope in the L*ORD *will renew their strength.*
They will soar on wings like eagles;
they will run and not grow weary,
they will walk and not be faint.
~ Isaiah 40:28–31

The clock's red numbers blinked. The time showed 4:00 a.m. This was the third day in a row I had awoken at the same annoying time. After an hour of trying to go back to sleep, I gave up and stumbled out of bed.

Stuffiness made my breathing difficult. Coughing hurt my chest as I shuffled to the kitchen for a cup of tea.

I sighed. *Sick again*. Since darkness kept me from enjoying the lake, I stayed inside for my daily devotional time. My hacking continued. Nausea came in waves.

I sighed. The previous day I had pruned poinsettias, pulled weeds, and dug up grass to enlarge flowerbeds, with plenty of energy left over. In one day, everything changed. My early walk from my bedroom to the kitchen wore me out.

Before dawn, I crawled back into bed. Under the covers, I shivered and wondered if I had the virus. Sleep came quickly.

By the time my eyes opened to the light, the bedside clock read 8:30 a.m., a very late hour for an early riser like me. I pulled my weary body out of bed.

After breakfast, I cleaned the kitchen easily and cleared my throat only occasionally. Stuffiness disappeared by midmorning. Perhaps I didn't have the dreaded disease but was exhausted from working in my yard.

As the day progressed, my energy increased and bothersome symptoms disappeared. My fears of contracting a deadly virus didn't materialize. Useless worry had robbed me of peace. Anxiety had taken away contentment when I took my focus off Jesus.

Lord, thank you for your protection, strength, and
healing. Help us focus on your love and faithfulness
instead of our anxieties.
Amen.

DAY 14: WEEKS OF QUARANTINE

*With every sun's rising, surprise us with Your love,
satisfy us with Your kindness. Then we will sing for joy and
celebrate every day we are alive.*
~ *Psalm 90:14 VOICE*

Two weeks of intense fatigue from bronchitis had kept me housebound. Just as I improved and looked forward to getting out, the pandemic added another period of isolation.

When energy returned, I eagerly attacked chores as I cleaned the house and garage. My yard looked better after I pulled weeds and trimmed plants. I read, finished craft projects, played games, texted friends, and sent encouraging cards.

Then my focus wavered. My to-do list mocked me. My mind formed plans, but my motivation and energy disappeared.

One morning, the peacefulness of the lake consoled me. Birdsong revitalized my concentration. Suddenly, boisterous screeching from one side of the serene water disturbed the tranquility. A bald eagle swooped from one treetop to another.

I grabbed my binoculars and focused on the majestic bird. A next-door neighbor appeared with her binoculars. As we scanned the lake, we noticed two adult eagles in separate pine trees. A young eagle perched at the edge of their nest. The little eaglet squealed and uttered desperate pleas for help. The nearby parents encouraged the youngster but didn't help him fly.

No matter how much the youngster cried out in protest, they stood firm on their perches. The adults forced him to leave the nest on his own. I didn't see the young one flee, but after several minutes, stillness returned.

From chaos to serenity, the episode revived me. Like the shrieking of the juvenile eagle, whining didn't change my situation. Instead of complaining about being home, I could make the most of forced isolation. I visited with my neighbors in our yards. On daily walks and bike rides, I encountered old friends and made new ones. My kitchen became a factory for baked goods that I shared with nearby friends.

Each day, we choose how to react to tough situations. Will there be whining or thankfulness?

Dear Lord, help us as we deal with difficult situations.
We know you are near even during the trials when we
feel alone. Help us sing for joy and be thankful.
Amen.

DAY 15: IS IT TRUE? IS IT KIND? IS IT HELPFUL?

I sought the Lord, and he answered me;
he delivered me from all my fears.
~ Psalm 34:4

As I heard and read numerous commentaries and tirades during the pandemic, I remembered words I heard long ago: Is it true? Is it kind? Is it helpful?

Solitude, loss of jobs, sickness, divorce, and uncertainty caused fear, frustration, and anger. Changes occurred daily. Unforeseen situations came often. Only a few remained who had experience coping with a worldwide pandemic.

Workers on the front lines faced unfathomable life-and-death situations that the rest of us could not imagine. Frustration at not being able to save patients, having limited supplies, and exposing themselves and their families to the virus caused constant psychological turmoil and physical stress.

Local, state, and national elected officials dealt tirelessly as they tried to make timely and appropriate decisions. Each leader attempted to make the best rulings with the given data, which vacillated day by day and even hour by hour. Like Monday-morning armchair coaches, many citizens felt they knew how to better lead each county, state, and the country.

Of course, many of the decisions caused controversy and polarized the nation. However, no one wanted a high national death toll or a plummeting economy. Problems occurred. Tempers flared. Most officials and medical professionals seemed to do the best they could with what they knew.

Amid trials, isn't it better to band together instead of criticizing and berating? Refrain from condemning? Encourage those who are making hard decisions? We all face hard times and can't escape that.

So, before posting or complaining, ask yourself, *Is it true? Is it kind? Is it helpful?*

When I was growing up, my parents would say, "If you can't say something nice, don't say anything at all." If we all did that, our world would be more peaceful. Social media would be less busy.

To counteract chaos, I listen to sermons, devotions, and music instead of becoming immersed in social media. Filling my mind with hope keeps me from obsessing on the dire news.

We will get through the present times by being united. We will emerge stronger. And if we work together, the journey will be smoother.

> *Dear Lord, take away our fears as we depend on you*
> *for peace and strength in overwhelming situations.*
> *Bring us together as families, communities, states, and*
> *a nation. Give the leaders wisdom and grace as they lead.*
> *Amen.*

DAY 16: PALM SUNDAY'S LATEST OPPRESSION

*Then, as He was now drawing near the descent of the Mount of
Olives, the whole multitude of the disciples began to praise God
with a loud voice for the mighty works they had seen, saying:
"'Blessed is the King who comes in the name of the LORD!
Peace in heaven and glory in the highest.'"
~ Luke 19:37–38 NKJV*

Little hands held palm branches and paraded through the sanctuary every year. I looked forward to the procession of young children who walked and danced to the music during Palm Sunday services.

Tiny youngsters could barely hold their branches. Older ones held palms high and confidently. A few swung fronds like swords. First-timers hung back when they saw the huge congregation.

Jubilation filled the church while youngsters played the part of Israelites leading Jesus into Jerusalem. Lush, green branches and cloaks lined his path. From the Mount of Olives down into the valley and then into the city, people praised their Messiah.

Memories from previous years filled my mind. But the shutdown made 2020's Palm Sunday quite different. I didn't get to watch my youngest granddaughter walk down the aisle for the last time holding her palm. Instead, our church service would be comprised of a slide show of congregants holding palm branches. In my front yard, a friend and I stood six feet apart with our fronds while her husband took our picture to add to the presentation.

Christians around the world celebrated differently as we all remembered the story of Jesus's descent into Jerusalem. Just like the people looked for a Savior to heal the sick and release them from Roman bondage, we prayed for healing. As in the past, people around the world prayed for a Redeemer to end oppression and misery.

As the pandemic continued to oppress the world, death lurked. Anxiety and fear seized hearts and minds. Like the crowd celebrating Jesus's entry into the city so many years ago, the present world looked for healing and release from the grip of the virus.

Even during isolation, Jesus offers hope, peace, and strength. That year, we weren't able to meet in-person for church, but thankfully we could watch church services on television and the internet. We could immerse ourselves in our Bibles, and in Christian books and music, which many countries don't have access to.

Even in the midst of the pandemic, we weren't defeated.

Father, thank you for sending Jesus to save us. Give us peace and hope as we worship you in our new and different ways.
Amen.

DAY 17: MAILBOX FRONDS

The next day the great crowd that had come for the festival heard that Jesus was on his way to Jerusalem. They took palm branches and went out to meet him, shouting, "Hosanna!"
"Blessed is he who comes in the name of the Lord!"
"Blessed is the king of Israel!"
Jesus found a young donkey and sat on it, as it is written:
"Do not be afraid, Daughter Zion see, your king is coming, seated on a donkey's colt."
~ John 12:12–15

As I grieved the loss of a long-held Palm Sunday tradition of the children parading through the church, a new one emerged. On Saturday evening, I attached palm fronds to my mailbox as a reminder of Jesus's final entry into Jerusalem.

The next morning, I planned to ride my pink bike through the neighborhood just after dawn to see how many others displayed their palms. While reading my devotionals before sunrise, I heard a familiar sound from the lake. Then the sun lit up the sky, and I saw gentle raindrops peppering the water.

The rain came like showers of blessings for our parched state. In the midst of a drought, the threat of wildfires loomed. Even though weather delayed my anticipated bike ride, we desperately needed the water.

Nothing about Palm Sunday was normal, but I discovered novel ways to worship. When the rain stopped, I rode my bright bicycle around the community. Several neighbors also displayed palm branches to commemorate the occasion. I even explained the significance of the greenery to questioning walkers who passed by.

Later, I watched my church's online service and other sermons on television. The different ways of commemorating Jesus's final entry into Jerusalem brought me joy even in difficult times.

Lord, even when we can't meet together to worship, you still show up. We can praise you at church or at home. Thank you for the rain and palm branches on mailboxes to celebrate Palm Sunday.
Amen.

DAY 18: TEARS OF SORROW

LORD, be gracious to us; we long for you. Be our strength every morning, our salvation in time of distress.
~ Isaiah 33:2

Like a dark cloak, sadness shrouded me. I missed talking and laughing with my husband, Alan. My heart longed to be with my family, friends, and Bible study friends. A deep void formed from the lack of fellowship. Not going to church and having normal interactions with people had affected me more profoundly than I realized.

For five weeks, I had been isolated and at home with only a few trips outside my neighborhood. I started working on projects to keep me busy, which helped me adapt to the seclusion.

When I awoke at 4:30 a.m., my mind wouldn't shut off. The magnitude of the pandemic seemed too overwhelming and the effects permeated every area of life. My ninety-six-year-old aunt and many others in assisted living facilities received no visitors or social activities. Other lonely widows battled depression. Some family members and friends worked in high-risk jobs. Families grieved as the death toll increased. Millions of people continued to be out of work. I wondered when or if there would ever be a sense of normalcy again.

As I walked across my dark bedroom, tears started. I didn't try to stop them. For weeks, I had avoided the oppression from my illness and isolation. Like a simmering volcano, sadness flowed in a stream of sorrow down my cheeks.

At 5:30 a.m., I turned on my computer and saw a devotional from Pastor Matt. He revisited his message from the previous Sunday, "Fear versus Hope." I exhaled. Just what I needed to hear.

When I moved to my patio, I thought of Jesus's last week of life. He felt sorrow and wept over Jerusalem. He prayed and cried out to God. He knew trusted friends would deny him. Judas, one of his disciples, would even betray him. But our Lord continued teaching, loving, and praying even while facing death.

Later, a walk outside revived me. I waved to and chatted with neighbors.

During my seclusion, I realized my need to stay connected to God, family, and friends. There will be times of sadness and loneliness in our lives that should be acknowledged, but they are not a place to reside. I was reminded that my dwelling place is with my Savior, not the world. My heavy heart felt lighter.

> *Heavenly Father, give us strength and peace*
> *as we continue to face the unknown.*
> *Amen.*

DAY 19: DARKNESS AND DESPAIR

Near the place He was crucified, there was a garden with a newly prepared tomb. Because it was the day of preparation, they arranged to lay Jesus in this tomb so they could rest on the Sabbath.
~ John 19:41–42 VOICE

The wind whipped through the trees before dawn. Darkness entombed the lake. Heavy clouds blocked the sun as light dissolved into the shadows. Waves rushed across the water.

The morning gloom seemed an appropriate setting to read of Jesus's mock trial, crucifixion, and burial. I read each of the Gospel accounts, from the Last Supper to his burial.

From celebrating on Palm Sunday to despair on Good Friday, Jesus's followers felt a full range of emotions. In less than a week, their lives went from hope and light to anguish and darkness with uncertainty for the future.

Good Friday appeared to be a ruthless and undeserving end to a promising and glorious life. Questions must have filled their minds and hearts. *What do we do now? Will we be killed too? Where do we go? Was Jesus lying?*

The pandemic posed similar questions. As we struggled to know what to believe, fear set in. *What do we do to be safe? Will we or our loved ones fall to the disease? How do we cope?*

My heart breaks for those who don't know Jesus and have fallen into a pit of despair. You see it in their eyes—dread, anxiety, and desperation.

However, for Christians who know the rest of the story, there is peace in the turmoil. Even though we experience fear, we feel comfort from the Light of our Savior. Life's journey is not easy or without questions, but ultimately we realize we aren't in control. God is.

Over time, Good Friday and the pandemic ended. As Easter approached, I also looked ahead in faith to the time when the virus would be but a memory. Thank you, Jesus, for saving me and giving me hope.

Loving Father, help us trust you in dark times just as we do in good times. Waiting is hard. Don't let us forget the lessons from our times of despair.
Amen.

DAY 20: MOURNFUL WAITING

"Peace be with you." They were startled and frightened, thinking they saw a ghost. [Jesus] said to them, "Why are you troubled, and why do doubts rise in your minds?"
~ Luke 24:36–38

Yesterday's sadness clutched my heart like a vise, but the pain lessened to a dull ache.

Good Friday brought mourning and despair to Jesus's followers too. Many fled the horrendous crucifixion to avoid seeing their teacher and friend killed like a common criminal. The finality of his battered body taken down from the rugged cross tore their hearts. The shattered dreams of their Lord as their earthly king weighed heavily on their hearts.

After Jesus died, his followers thought it was over. They didn't wait expectantly on Saturday, but fearfully hid in locked rooms. Although Jesus had told them about his resurrection in three days, they didn't understand.

Every year, in remembrance of this historic event, Christians around the world pause and reflect on Jesus's death. But what about twenty-four hours later? This often-overlooked somber day brought contemplation. Normally, we prepare for Easter on Saturday. Over two thousand years ago, Jesus's disciples and followers didn't know their Savior would rise from the dead a few hours later. Like us, they were shrouded in darkness. A return to a normal life seemed like a dream.

Like the disciples, no one knew what would come next with the pandemic. *Will the virus get worse? When will it end? Will businesses reopen? What will schools do?* Questions abounded with few answers.

Thankfully, for Christians, Jesus's resurrection still brings joy and hope. After Good Friday and Somber Saturday, we know the joy of Easter comes. Despite what happens in our world, God is in control and knows the plan.

Father, you know the rest of the story. Give us peace and remove our fears as we deal with stressful situations. Thank you for loving us even when we doubt.
Amen.

DAY 21: THE FINAL EASTER PICTURE

Now as they said these things, Jesus Himself stood in the midst of them, and said to them, "Peace to you."
~ Luke 24:36 NKJV

"Send us your Easter pictures," our pastor encouraged us during our weekly online service. The church website reminded us to dress up, take pictures, and send them so we could see each other on Easter.

It seemed strange to put on a colorful dress and cosmetics after months of staying home in shorts and t-shirts with no makeup. With the absence of new clothes for the celebration, I chose a pink dress and my favorite sandals from my closet.

Friends came to my house so we could take a group shot by the lake. Nancy, Maura, and Maura's husband, Chuck, who was our photographer, arrived at my home just after lunch. In the perfect afternoon sunlight, we walked to the back of my house for our picture.

After her mom passed away, Maura had kept her mom's extensive hat collection. Memories of her mom made

Maura's eyes sparkle as she handed Nancy and me each a special chapeau as a sweet reminder of her mom's life.

With beautiful Easter bonnets perched on our heads, we stood near the shore. Breezes brushed our faces and ruffled our hair. Nancy's dress flowed around her but did little to conceal her thin figure. A smile lit up her face despite the pain she endured from cancer and its brutal treatments.

As we celebrated Jesus's death, resurrection, and ascension, we all realized that Nancy would soon join Jesus in heaven.

While Chuck took pictures, we smiled, laughed, and enjoyed our time of celebration. For a few minutes, we put aside the agony, cancer treatments, and impending death of one of our dear friends. Each of us relished the moment we shared.

At the end of her life, Nancy stayed with Chuck and Maura in their home so they could nurture and care for her. A few months after Easter, Nancy left us to be with Jesus. We rejoice in the knowledge that she is now free from cancer and pain.

Our Easter picture now resides in several states so that Nancy's family and friends can remember her beautiful smile and the extraordinary life she lived.

Loving Father, thank you for coming to save us and giving us peace even in our grief.
Amen.

DAY 22: A NOVEL EASTER SUNRISE

On the first day of the week, very early in the morning, the women took the spices they had prepared and went to the tomb. They found the stone rolled away from the tomb, but when they entered, they did not find the body of the Lord Jesus. While they were wondering about this, suddenly two men in clothes that gleamed like lightning stood beside them. In their fright the women bowed down with their faces to the ground, but the men said to them, "Why do you look for the living among the dead? He is not here; he has risen! Remember how he told you, while he was still with you in Galilee: 'The Son of Man must be delivered over to the hands of sinners, be crucified and on the third day be raised again.'" Then they remembered his words.
~ Luke 24:1–8

I gave up trying to go back to sleep. The clock read 5:00 a.m. My mind replayed the tasks I had planned for the day.

After a cup of tea, I grabbed some maroon ribbon and pink artificial flowers, then walked outside. I knelt before the magnolia branch cross I had made for Good Friday. Gently, I removed the somber black cloth that circled the crossbeams.

Gold-flecked dark-red ribbon adorned the cross. Pink flowers woven into a bow crowned the Easter decoration and symbolized new birth. After dawn, walkers and bikers would be able to see the cross that symbolized Easter.

I hummed "The Old Rugged Cross," one of my dad's favorite hymns, as I walked in the dark to nearby homes. I sang about the cross and thought of the women who went to Jesus's tomb in the dark early on Easter morning. With broken hearts, they carried the burial spices and oils to anoint his shattered body. They didn't know the surprise and joy that awaited them.

I joyfully repeated that hymn in the blackness because I knew the blessedness of Jesus's resurrection. At each house along my street, I left a plastic egg filled with candy and a note, "Happy Easter. He has risen."

As the sun rose, I "attended" my first Easter service online that day. My son Chris preached. His words touched my heart. I watched friends from my church welcome worshipers online. Our praise team sang meaningful songs.

Normally, our church would be filled with worshipers in colorful, new clothes. Instead, as I solemnly watched online, I received an awakening in my heart to the true meaning of Easter. Worshiping alone with fewer distractions helped me focus on the sermon and the significance of Easter. Even though the morning didn't follow my "normal" Easter traditions, excitement filled my heart.

Savior, thank you for loving us so much that you would die for us. We rejoice at your resurrection.
Amen.

DAY 23: WONDROUS EASTER AT HOME

When the Sabbath was over, Mary Magdalene, Mary the mother of James, and Salome bought spices so that they might go to anoint Jesus' body. Very early on the first day of the week, just after sunrise, they were on their way to the tomb and they asked each other, "Who will roll the stone away from the entrance of the tomb?" But when they looked up, they saw that the stone, which was very large, had been rolled away. As they entered the tomb, they saw a young man dressed in a white robe sitting on the right side, and they were alarmed. "Don't be alarmed," he said. "You are looking for Jesus the Nazarene, who was crucified.
He has risen! He is not here.
See the place where they laid him. But go, tell his disciples and Peter, 'He is going ahead of you into Galilee. There you will see him, just as he told you.'"
~ Mark 16:1–8

After watching a couple of church services online, I hopped on my trusty bike to deliver the remaining Easter eggs to friends throughout the neighborhood. I giggled to myself as I laid an egg on each doorstep.

A while later at home, I took a tour of my yard. Dressed in their Easter finery, one splendid flower after another greeted me. Birds sang captivating melodies. A majestic bald eagle circled the lake. Several chrysalises hung from the top of my butterfly cage waiting for their transformation into monarch butterflies.

Neighbors joined me as we watched a pair of regal sandhill cranes lead their youngsters to the shore. Their downy yellow bodies reminded us of a larger version of baby chicks.

All around me, God revealed the message of his resurrection story within creation. A quiet day of contemplation provided a unique, meaningful Easter.

Although I still missed being with my family and friends at church, my heart smiled when my phone rang and my granddaughter Emily wished me a happy Easter. Instead of talking like she usually did, she said she would call back, which seemed strange.

I decided to enjoy the weather. When I stepped onto the porch, from the corner of my eye I noticed movement. After being secluded for so long, it seemed like a mirage. My son, his wife, and my three granddaughters stood only a few feet from me.

Joy filled my heart. Tears threatened. I wanted to run over and hug them all, but social distancing kept us apart. We talked and joked as I tried to process the reality of them actually being in my yard. Before they left, I took a picture of them to remind myself of the incredible gift.

Their visit was the perfect ending to an unexpected yet momentous Easter.

Jesus, thank you for dying for us and for our seeing you in unexpected ways during an exceptional Easter.
Amen.

DAY 24: MONARCH MIRACLES

I will offer You my grateful heart, for I am Your unique creation, filled with wonder and awe. You have approached even the smallest details with excellence; Your works are wonderful; I carry this knowledge deep within my soul.
~ *Psalm 139:14 VOICE*

Teeny white dots clung to the underside of milkweed leaves. My youngest granddaughter pointed out almost microscopic butterfly eggs. Without her direction, I would have missed them.

After a few days, rice-sized creatures hatched from the eggs. Only with careful observation did I see the teensy caterpillars. Soon they turned into yellow, white, green, and black striped larvae. Several times a day I watched them creep all over the milkweed plants as they devoured leaves.

When they were a little larger, I moved them into my butterfly cages to protect them from predators. Every day, the larvae munched and fattened up after devouring the plants.

After days of eating voraciously, each larva climbed to the

top of the cage, hung upside down, and formed a chrysalis. Every creature miraculously squeezed itself into a small, green chrysalis wrapped with a gold ring around the middle.

Ten to fourteen days later, the green chrysalises turned black. At just the right time, a delicate, winged insect unfolded itself. Bit by bit, the fluid coursed through the wings in a miraculous presentation that took my breath away. When fully expanded, the wings fluttered, rested, and then flapped with their full strength.

All summer, my neighbor and I worked together to release monarchs. Often, they flew from side to side in the cage, but we learned how to entice them to land on our fingers. Some took off at once. A few flew to flowers and then disappeared. A couple with deformed wings remained close. We tried to help them, but they died or were eaten.

During their two-week life span, females laid more eggs and the cycle continued. Every insect went through the same stages. Each one developed into a butterfly with the same exact colors and detailed design. The wondrous life cycle amazed me every time I observed the metamorphosis.

God's creation contains millions of astounding miracles, but in my normally busy schedule, I would have never had the luxury of immersing myself into the raising of monarchs.

The butterfly transformation is a metaphor for our changed lives. Every person begins life as a microscopic being that becomes a marvelous creature capable of astounding feats. Since God took so much care to create an enchanting butterfly, imagine how meticulously he crafted each human being.

Every one of us is fearfully and wonderfully made.

Loving Father, thank you for creating us with so much love and creativity. Each person is unique and special in your eyes.
Amen.

DAY 25: CONFLICTING ALERTS

*I lift up my eyes to the mountains—
where does my help come from?
My help comes from the L*ORD*, the Maker of heaven and earth.
He will not let your foot slip—
he who watches over you will not slumber.
~ Psalm 121:1–3*

As I tried to fall back asleep, my phone pinged. Normally, calls and messages are silenced until 7:00 a.m., so my curiosity propelled me from my bed. A weather alert proclaimed a severe thunderstorm warning for my area. At least it wasn't a tornado watch like earlier in the week.

Even though it was early, I fixed a cup of tea and headed outside. An ebony cloak surrounded my patio so nothing showed up beyond the screen. The wind rustled trees as I wrote in my gratitude journal and read daily devotionals. Lightning flashed closer and closer.

A stiff gale rushed through my patio. Rain pelted the roof and dripped down the screens. Thunder rumbled. Another weather alert popped up on my phone notifying me that there were no longer storms in my area. My eyes and ears disagreed.

As the storm intensified, I moved inside to check the Weather Channel on my TV. It showed thunderstorms over my town and a tornado watch for five more hours. How could my phone alert be so different from the Weather Channel's report?

Finally, the rain slowed. Rolling thunder and flashes of light moved away. A gray dawn crept across the lake.

Weather alarms and my own limited observations clashed. Even though I tried to find a clear answer, none came.

Likewise, I would have loved to have a definite answer to the end of my seclusion. When would I be able to visit my family? Go out to lunch with friends? Invite people into my home?

However, just as I couldn't see into the dark morning, I couldn't see into the future. I still can't, and no one else can either. Predictions can be made, but they don't always come true.

God sees the whole picture when I only see a tiny slice. It is easy to worry about what is coming, but better to trust that God has it under control.

Lord, give us peace as we endure uncertainty. Help us trust you as our protector who never sleeps.
Amen.

DAY 26: WHERE IS YOUR FOCUS?

The LORD is my strength and my shield;
my heart trusts in him, and he helps me.
My heart leaps for joy,
and with my song
I praise him.
~ Psalm 28:7

One butterfly hung from the top of the cage next to four pupas. I had no idea when the others would emerge.

An hour later, when I checked on the butterfly, his wings were proudly flapping and he was making trial flights around the enclosure.

Another monarch had emerged but now lay sideways on the bottom of the cage. His wee legs fluttered in the air. He couldn't right himself. I gently put my finger near him without touching his fragile wings. After several attempts, he weakly grasped my finger and then gripped the mesh at the top of the cage. When I took my hand away, he fell to the floor again.

For a couple of hours, the two insects flapped their wings and filled them with fluid. They seemed ready to be released into the outside world.

I called to my neighbor to join me for the release ceremony, and she promptly dropped her gardening tools and came over. Gently, she inched her finger inside while I held the habitat waist high. The stronger creature latched onto her finger and then zoomed away.

With much effort, the weaker one attached to her finger. Once outside the cage, he dropped to our feet, so we were afraid he would not survive. We watched as he flew a few feet and dropped again. Up and down he went. Finally, with a renewed burst of energy, he took off in flight.

Eighteen chrysalises hatched during my initial season of butterfly nurturing, but two never opened. I couldn't take responsibility for the eighteen perfect ones nor the two failures. Even so, I had a choice. I could rejoice with the healthy ones that flitted around my garden or ignore them and feel hopeless for the lost ones.

I found power in my perspective. Focusing on fear brings depression and sadness. Concentrating on blessings brings joy.

Every day, I choose joy.

Loving Father, even in the midst of turmoil and losses,
we can find joy and thankfulness.
Amen.

DAY 27: GOD'S ASTOUNDING GIFTS

The heavens declare the glory of God;
the skies proclaim the work of his hands.
Day after day they pour forth speech;
night after night they reveal knowledge.
They have no speech, they use no words;
no sound is heard from them.
Yet their voice goes out into all the earth,
their words to the ends of the world.
In the heavens God has pitched a tent for the sun.
~ Psalm 19:1–4

Hues of pink were painted across the eastern sky when I stepped onto my patio. The beauty of the morning captured my attention.

Before starting my morning devotions, I looked into my butterfly enclosure. Two plump, striped caterpillars clung to the top of the cage. The three milkweed plants I had given them the previous day had been stripped of their leaves. I pulled out the empty stems and exchanged them for fuller ones.

A variety of birds chirped and sang. I tilted my head and closed my eyes to let their joyful songs envelop me. An eagle interrupted their melody with his unpleasant screeching.

The bald eagle soared above and landed on the shoreline. Scanning the lake with his powerful, beady dark eyes, he watched the waters ripple and then dunked his stately head into the water. After a shake, he lifted his powerful wings and flew to a tall pine tree with a wriggling fish in his talons. His dark feathered body blended in with the forest, but his white crown stood out like a beacon of light.

My gaze turned back toward the middle of the lake, where a large fish leaped into the air and landed with a splash. Waves rippled out across the mirrored pond.

Two of my devotional readings that day focused on the wonders of creation. One wrote that God provides a wondrous creation for His glory and for us to enjoy. The second one reminded me of the majesty of God's creation and how he speaks to us through it.

Each one touched my heart as I watched the morning unfold. From my patio, I enjoyed watching numerous creatures, from creeping caterpillars to magnificent eagles. Towering trees and tiny flowers enhanced my view. Spectacular sunrises and sunsets painted the sky.

Everything we see and hear in nature points to our God and Creator.

Creator, we marvel at the majesty and
handiwork we see all around us.
Amen.

DAY 28: MISSING ANOTHER MIRACLE

Jesus said to them,
"My Father is always at his work to this very day,
and I too am working."
~ John 5:17

Not again. Hour after hour, I knelt on my patio floor to examine the small butterfly cage that held two monarch caterpillars. One hung from the top, which signaled it was preparing to form a chrysalis. The second larva crawled along the side with its threadlike black legs.

As day turned into evening, I had trouble finding the brightly striped caterpillar as the plastic top of the cage blurred my view. Finally, I found him. His long body began to darken in color, compressing into a tiny version of himself.

I went onto my patio after dinner to check on his progress, longing to watch the larva spin a small, green chrysalis around its body. Before bed, I made one last trip outside. Nothing had changed.

Just after dawn the next day, I walked to my porch and looked down at the butterfly cage. A green chrysalis hung snugly to the top. I had again missed the miracle of transformation.

Even though I didn't get to see the conversion from larva to pupa eighteen times, I marveled at the results of metamorphosis every time. The beauty and intricacy of the Lord's creation filled me with wonder and awe.

God's miracles occur all around me. Seeds become exquisite flowers. Bare cypress trees fill out in waves of green. Eagles lay eggs and hatch tiny reproductions of themselves. I don't observe the entire process of those changes either, but the results astonish me.

God transforms messy lives into grand masterpieces.

Dear Father, you are constantly performing miracles in your world. Help us look for the small and big ones every day.
Amen.

DAY 29: CHRYSALIS OF LIFE

Now listen, you who say, "Today or tomorrow we will go to this or that city, spend a year there, carry on business and make money." Why, you do not even know what will happen tomorrow. What is your life? You are a mist that appears for a little while and then vanishes. Instead, you ought to say, "If it is the Lord's will, we will live and do this or that."
~ James 4:13–15

Before my husband, Alan, transformed from this life to eternity, people prayed for his healing, but he didn't get better physically.

The doctor predicted Alan had six months to live, but he continued living fully. After we got home that day, instead of lamenting his upcoming death, he began a long list of things to accomplish. Calls ensued to the insurance company to check on his life insurance, he purchased a new car and bike for me, and he even set up a scholarship fund at Luther College.

I marveled at his tenacity. Nothing on the list was for himself; everything he did was for others—to make my life and others' lives easier after he passed. At the time, my heart ached with each checked-off and completed item.

He openly and bravely shared his faith and peace with family members, friends, and even the man who delivered oxygen to him. During that time, I watched his faith deepen as he moved closer to heaven.

Only later did I realize how much he prepared for his departure, and for me to live without him. His certainty of being with Jesus gave me peace and strength during my initial time of grief, and it continues. Since that time, God has continually placed people in my life who are grieving so I can comfort them the way I was comforted.

The miracle God was working in me while Alan was alive wasn't obvious at the time. However, later I could see how God orchestrated another miracle as part of his plan.

Dear Father, you are constantly caring for us, even during our darkest times. Help us see your hand at work even when we walk through the valley of the shadow of death.
Amen.

DAY 30: CONTENTMENT DURING THE STORMS

*I am not saying this because I am in need,
for I have learned to be content whatever the circumstances.
I know what it is to be in need, and I know what it is to have
plenty. I have learned the secret of being content in any and every
situation, whether well fed or hungry,
whether living in plenty or in want.
I can do all this through him who gives me strength.
~ Philippians 4:11–13*

Gusts of wind bent trees and blew rain across my patio. The torrents beat my windows in the early hours before dawn, then slowed for the remainder of the day. Cool breezes brushed the lake. Light rain continued under a slate sky as the thirsty ground sucked up all the rainwater.

The weather kept me from my daily walking and bike riding throughout the neighborhood. Dreariness shrouded my home like a gigantic cape. Daylight barely lightened the lake. But my snug, cocoon blanket provided warmth and safety.

It was the perfect day to tackle more items on my to-do list. Bags of clothes from my closet and books from my library would find new homes. In the afternoon, enjoying another book brought pleasure.

Even on gorgeous days, adjusting to a slower pace brought contentment. More research on monarch butterflies took hours, and I included a few neighbors in my project. Yard work strengthened my muscles and improved my flower gardens. Walking and riding my bike throughout the neighborhood reduced blood pressure and helped me interact with people. Friends came over, and we played games outside.

Old hobbies brought enjoyment as I crocheted hats and dishcloths to give away. Playing my keyboard filled my home with music. There was no time to be depressed or bored. Instead of becoming distressed, I thanked God for his provision and care.

When required to stay home, even on dreary days, there are always opportunities to relax, learn, and explore.

Dear Lord, sometimes it is good to slow down and appreciate the time of rest. We can learn to be content in our circumstances and enjoy the blessings around us. Thank you for being with us in good times and difficult ones.
Amen.

DAY 31: TRUSTING GOD FOR MOTHER'S DAY

Now he who supplies see to the sower and bread for food will also supply and increase your store of seed and will enlarge the harvest of your righteousness. You will be enriched in every way so that you can be generous on every occasion, and through us your generosity will result in thanksgiving to God.
~ 2 Corinthians 9:10–11

Last year, our women's club gathered to prepare bags of Mother's Day gifts for residents of an assisted living facility. We also provided gift bags for the moms in a transitional housing establishment for families with young children. As the leader of our outreach committee, I organized these outreaches to provide presents on special occasions.

Then isolation changed our plans.

Residents of my neighborhood donated items during the year, but with no in-person meetings, we only received a quarter of our usual contributions. I hoped there would be an ample supply of gifts in our clubhouse closet from previous drives.

I called the club manager to see if I could access our storage area. He said I could come to the closed clubhouse, but unfortunately he couldn't find the closet key. He assured me that he would contact me as soon as he found it.

For three days, I waited. No call. I stayed home, not wanting to go out to shop with the virus still a problem. My thoughts raced as I thought of all the needed gifts for the mothers at the facilities.

This affected my sleep. Way before dawn, I plodded to the kitchen for a cup of tea. During my devotional time, God whispered for me to trust him.

Later that morning, in faith, I called the manager and left a message.

My phone rang after lunch. "I found the key. You can come up alone to check the closet."

I hurried to the almost-empty clubhouse, where two masked staff members greeted me. "Thank you so much. Now I won't have to go shopping," I said, opening the partially filled closet.

Donations from generous residents filled my trunk. Because of the pandemic, no one could help me assemble bags with shampoo, lotion, tissues, sanitizer, and candy like in previous years. Although we couldn't personally hand out presents and offer encouragement, God provided gifts for twenty mothers.

The following day, I woke up early, not from worry but from excitement of giving to those who might have felt lonely and forgotten.

God had reminded me again to trust in his provisions and timing.

Jehovah-Jireh, "The Lord Will Provide," thank you for patiently teaching us to trust that you will provide in your time and not ours.
Amen.

DAY 32: BLESSING IN COMMUNITY

Let us consider how to inspire each other to greater love and to righteous deeds, not forgetting to gather as a community, as some have forgotten, but encouraging each other, especially as the day of His return approaches.
~ Hebrews 10:24–25 VOICE

Like beacons of light, my orchids burst forth with color. They hung on a wooden plant tower with clusters of blooms on long stems.

Each plant produced a unique color, size, and design. Large white blooms with yellow centers covered one plant. Another produced rich, velvety mauve flowers. Beige blossoms striped with violet graced the third pot. Tiny purple blooms, etched with white, covered the fourth plant.

Up close, I examined them and was amazed at the intricate design of every variety. The flowers on each stem were exactly the same but different from the other plants even though they were all orchids.

Once a week, I watered them and occasionally added fertilizer. They received morning sunshine and shade from intense afternoon rays. Even though I provided favorable growing conditions, nothing I did made them grow. Only God does that. He created every one of them and determines its size, color, and design.

The gorgeous orchids bloom once a year, usually lasting for months. Although every flower is unique and lovely, the collection provides a splendid arrangement.

In community, we also flourish as we help each other. As a group, we can serve, share, and produce more than we can individually. During isolation, we appreciate how family members, Bible study groups, neighbors, and colleagues all contribute to our mental, spiritual, and physical well-being.

Bonds formed in community help us flourish as we serve and love others.

Father, help us inspire and encourage each other to use our gifts and talents. Thank you for the blessing of community.
Amen.

DAY 33: RETURNING TO MY PINK BIKE

Not only so, but we also glory in our sufferings, because we know that suffering produces perseverance; perseverance, character; and character, hope. And hope does not put us to shame, because God's love has been poured out into our hearts through the Holy Spirit, who has been given to us.
~ *Romans 5:3–5*

The pink bike Alan bought me shortly before he died stood forlornly in my garage. I tried not to look at it because I then remembered when I used to ride around the entire neighborhood. Before bronchitis, I biked without getting out of breath easily and becoming dizzy.

But after weeks of easy walking, I needed a change in my routine. I pulled my bike out of the garage and started down the street. It felt good to be back on the seat with fresh air brushing my face. For a couple of blocks, I felt wonderful.

Then I huffed like a runner at the end of a marathon. Pumping my pedals up a slight incline seemed like climbing Mt. Everest. My home just down the street appeared miles away. When I returned home, the bike went into the garage and I flopped down on the couch.

Even though it was exhausting, every day I walked or rode my bike. Neighbors greeted me. Seeing them out encouraged me to continue. On biking days, older ladies passed me as I barely crept along. Intense bikers lapped me over and over as they sped through the neighborhood. However, each day I went a little farther on my bike. One mile turned into two. Bit by bit my stamina increased.

No longer did everyone pass me. I struggled to breathe only when really exerting myself. My rubbery legs became firm as my muscles grew. Discouragement dissipated.

Exercising forced me to get outside, which energized me physically, mentally, and emotionally even though I was still alone.

Heavenly Father, even in our suffering, we should persevere and move forward. You strengthen us as we build character, which produces hope.
Amen.

DAY 34: PRESSING TOWARD THE GOAL

Not that I have already obtained all this, or have already been made perfect, but I press on to take hold of that for which Christ Jesus took hold of me. Brothers, I do not consider myself yet to have taken hold of it. But one thing I do: Forgetting what is behind and straining toward what is ahead, I press on toward the goal to win the prize for which God has called me heavenward in Christ Jesus.
~ Philippians 3:12–14

Perched on my bright-pink bike, I pulled out of the garage for an early morning ride. The breeze ruffled my hair as I rode up and down vacant, shady streets near my home.

Every few minutes, I looked down at my Apple watch to check my time and distance. Two miles and then three. Watching the mileage motivated me to try completing four miles.

My legs pumped with renewed strength. I surpassed my goal of four miles and made it to four and a half. My heart rate increased, but I kept pedaling past my home and circled the block a few times to get to five miles. When I pulled into my driveway, I stopped the watch at five and three-tenths miles.

For me, that was a huge accomplishment. When my isolation began, bronchitis kept me down for two weeks. Strength returned little by little. Walks and bike rides brought on extreme shortness of breath. Going half a mile wore me out. Nevertheless, I persisted with walking or biking almost every day.

Cooler temperatures made exercising easier. While I biked, I waved and greeted neighbors who passed by. On walks, I talked to other residents and listened to sermon podcasts that compelled me to walk until the sermon finished. Improvements in my time and distance motivated me to not quit.

Daily exercise produced more energy and awakened my sense of thankfulness for God's creation around me. Podcasts of Christian speakers fed my soul and kept me moving spiritually and physically. Interacting with friends helped me deal with the loneliness of solitude.

Although separation can bring pain and loss, we can discover untried possibilities.

Father, help us not yearn for the past but press on toward the ultimate goal ahead of us.
Amen.

DAY 35: FINDING JOY AND PURPOSE

*The one who listens to me, who carefully seeks me in everyday
things and delays action until my way is apparent,
that one will find true happiness.*
~ Proverbs 8:34 VOICE

Swirling mist blurred vibrant reflections on the mirrored lake. Minutes later, little clouds dissipated and an upside-down forest glowed on the water.

Cypress limbs, heavy with overnight rain, drooped like weary travelers. Water diamonds gathered on the patio screen and waited to twinkle in the sunlight. A couple of trees in the forest radiated with a brilliant green, but shadows subdued the rest of the woods.

Despite the somber mood, cheerful birds sang melodic tunes. A spider web glistened with dew as it stretched from one limb to another.

Isolation had brought changes. For months, I stayed home alone. Normal activities stopped, but I discovered uplifting shows on television. My car rested, but my bike usage surged. Walking provided daily exercise.

During the shutdown, my time enjoying nature from my patio increased. A variety of birds appeared daily, from tiny hummingbirds to majestic eagles. An abundance of vivid flowers graced my garden. My time with God each morning became richer and more bountiful as my faith grew.

After days of jumping from one activity to another with little focus, I wrote a lengthy to-do list. Gradually, the list grew smaller. Along with chores like cleaning the garage and purging files, I read a variety of books and pulled out special pencils to color in my adult coloring book. Leisurely days continued for several weeks.

Then Zoom entered my life with three Bible studies, writers' group meetings, writing critique sessions, and board meetings. Local charities needed supplies, so I donned my homemade mask and ventured out to brave the virus. After weeks of free time, suddenly I needed a schedule again.

When the sun rose and light replaced shadows, life around the lake changed. Likewise, opening up our country took me into a different phase. Living in isolation restyled my life in both positive and negative ways. Although I missed being with family and friends, I enjoyed a less complicated way of living.

Decisions awaited. *Will I return to an often-hectic schedule or cut back on some activities? Will I continue pursuits I actually enjoy or hang on to stressful obligations? Will I remove the insignificant to concentrate on the significant?*

In seclusion, I realized what was most important: praying for wisdom and direction, reading the Bible, enjoying people I treasure, and serving with the love of Jesus. God takes it all and weaves something beautiful.

Loving Father, when we seek you, the way becomes apparent. Thank you for working in our lives and revealing your plan for us even in the midst of change and uncertainty. Amen.

DAY 36: WAITING ON MY BREAD

Don't run from tests and hardships, brothers and sisters. As difficult as they are, you will ultimately find joy in them; if you embrace them, your faith will blossom under pressure and teach you true patience as you endure. And true patience brought on by endurance will equip you to complete the long journey and cross the finish line—mature, complete, and wanting nothing.
~ *James 1:2–4 VOICE*

Rain shortened my early morning walk. All day, I watched drops hit the lake. Clouds covered the sky like a heavy quilt.

Although the precipitation continued and kept me inside, I found plenty of tasks to accomplish. Dreariness produced a sense of comfort, so I snuggled with my fuzzy blanket on my couch with a book.

A little while later, my mom's bread machine enticed me. Ingredients for oat bread lined my counter. Flour, yeast, water, oats, and butter went into the metal container. I pushed buttons to begin the process. Kneading began with a hum and then a period of rest.

Three hours later, the aroma of freshly baked bread filled my home. Because the machine hadn't been used in several years, I didn't trust the timer. Twice, I opened the lid to check on it. Over and over, I looked through the glass top to see if the dough had finished baking. Impatiently, I waited for the beep to signal the bread was done.

Although the smell beckoned me to gobble up a piece of bread immediately, I remembered details from the instruction booklet. Take bread out of machine. Turn it over onto a wire rack. Let it cool before slicing.

Anxiously, I waited and watched the lightly browned loaf. I tried to stay busy with household tasks. The alluring scent tempted me, but I resisted.

Finally, I cut a small piece of the captivating creation. With a touch of butter and berry jelly from a friend, the warm treat melted in my mouth. Later in the day, I enjoyed another slice before sharing part of the loaf with friends.

If I had taken the bread out of the machine early, it would have been doughy and inedible. Before the bread cooled, the knife would have squashed the loaf into a lumpy mess. The delay challenged me, but the final product was well worth the wait.

Being alone often causes impatience and anxiety to escalate. But remembering that our loving Father is in control helped me reduce my nervousness.

God's timetable is usually not the same as ours. We need to read his instruction book, the Bible, for the best results. And trust him when we are required to wait.

Father, waiting on you produces patience and better outcomes than when we try to take over.
Amen.

DAY 37: RELEASED FROM MY CAGE

Satisfy us in the morning with your unfailing love, that we may sing for joy and be glad all our days.
~ Psalm 90:14

My car and I joined the rush of traffic on the interstate. For over three months, I had been sequestered at home with only occasional local jaunts near my house. Now, impatient drivers wove from one side of the road to the other and ignored the speed limit. My car stayed in the right lane away from the racetrack.

An ambulance passed by. More flashing lights came into view and then disappeared. Ahead of me, a group of police cars joined the emergency vehicles on the side of the road. A crowd stood near them, but there was no evidence of an accident.

Everything along my route seemed new and exciting. An Amazon distribution center had sprung up during my isolation. Rows of cars filled spaces at the mall. New apartment buildings sprouted in empty fields. A line of cars wound around McDonald's. Diners sat inside.

It surprised me that while I had stayed caged up at home, many people didn't. Construction workers erected buildings. Food service workers prepared meals. First responders kept our communities safe. Life went on somewhat normally for large groups of people.

When I pulled up to my son's home, my youngest granddaughter, Molly, opened the door. Her smiling face warmed my heart. In the kitchen, her sisters, Ashlyn and Emily, made cookies. What a joy to see my family.

All three granddaughters had grown taller during my absence. The two older girls had become young women.

Everything I experienced during that excursion seemed unfamiliar and memorable. Because of the confinement, I couldn't wait to see my family and give them hugs. Instead of ignoring houses, businesses, and forests during the short trip, I looked at everything with fresh eyes and a heartfelt appreciation.

Blessings come in all kinds of packages.

Loving Father, teach us to sing and be joyful for the love and kindness you give us every day.
Amen.

DAY 38: AN ALTERED ADVENTURE

*In their hearts humans plan their course,
but the L<small>ORD</small> establishes their steps.*
~ Proverbs 16:9

"Grandma, what are we going to do?" ten-year old Molly asked as we settled into my car.

The pandemic had separated us for months, but with restrictions lifting, she had decided to spend the night with me. After she hugged her mom and put her bulging suitcase in my trunk, our adventure began.

"We will get lunch somewhere. I have donations to drop off for a charity first."

Because the stop was close to downtown, I decided to take a different exit off the interstate than the one near my home.

Immersed in chatting and laughing with my delightful Molly, we sped by our intended off-ramp. "Oh no. I missed our turnoff," I said.

The next exit was nine miles away.

"Grandma, I'm hungry," she told me. "I didn't eat much for breakfast."

"We'll get something soon. Think of this as an adventure."

When we finally got off the interstate, I had to turn around to get back on the highway. My plan for a shorter trip actually took us longer.

"Grandma, we've been gone an hour."

"Not quite." I didn't want to admit that she was right.

We finally dropped off the donations and went through the drive-thru at a fast-food restaurant. At home, we opened the bag.

Molly unwrapped a warm package from the bag. "This has lettuce, so it must be yours." She opened another one, then scowled. "This one is chicken."

I sighed. We had ordered two hamburgers, one with lettuce and one without. "You can have mine."

"That's okay," she answered.

We ate limp fries with sandwiches we didn't order or really like.

Molly and I laughed at our detour and ate our less-than-perfect lunch enjoying each other's company much more than our food. Her enthusiasm and acceptance inspired me to not take life so seriously.

When plans don't turn out the way we want, we can whine about it or joyfully accept the detours.

Loving Father, during times of isolation, we can experience many changes, losses, and trials. Help us accept our disruptions graciously and remember you plan each one of our steps.
Amen.

DAY 39: SMALL BUT POWERFUL

Do not forget to rejoice, for hope is always just around the corner. Hold up through the hard times that are coming, and devote yourselves to prayer. Share what you have with the saints, so they lack nothing; take every opportunity to open your life and home to others. If people mistreat or malign you, bless them. Always speak blessings, not curses. If some have cause to celebrate, join in the celebration. And if others are weeping, join in that as well. Work toward unity, and live in harmony with one another. Avoid thinking you are better than others or wiser than the rest; instead, embrace common people and ordinary tasks.
~ *Romans 12:12–16 VOICE*

A string of tiny solar lights wrapped a tall wooden plant stand on my patio. At night, they twinkled in the darkness, but during the day, nothing about the plain green strands stood out. They dangled lifelessly from the top of the four-foot pole.

Sunlight streamed through the trees and onto my patio. A glittering surprise caught my attention. Spider webs filled in spaces between the lights. Intricate designs created a silky masterpiece.

A busy spider or family of them wove webs from one plant to another. Crisscrossing jeweled strands joined pots of aloe at the top to the herbs at the bottom with lovely lacework. These diligent workers must have spent hours and hours constructing the artistic designs.

Day after day, I sat in my comfy chair next to the plants to read my Bible, pray, and pore over my devotionals. Each morning, the lake beyond my yard greeted me with wildlife. Egrets, bald eagles, turkeys, and deer visited. Although admiring the beauty outside my patio, I had missed the marvelous creations next to me.

During the uncertainty of the pandemic, unrest from the protests, and turbulence of the riots, I searched the media for glimpses of hope. I wanted to see our leaders guide us through these global tragedies. I felt helpless and wondered what one person could do.

God spoke to me through his Word and a dear friend. Looking backward doesn't solve problems. We need to look ahead and make positive changes.

I had the power to pray for peaceful change and understanding. I could offer hope and encouragement to those around me who were in turmoil. Thank those who helped me. Listen more than I spoke. Instead of waiting for someone more prominent than me to solve the difficulties, I could make a difference in those near me.

The wee spiders did what they were made to do in a small way, and made such a powerful impact. If we could all do that, what a difference we could collectively make.

Loving Father, help us rejoice in hope, endure in trouble, and pray fervently.
Amen.

DAY 40: AN UNSEEN WORLD

"For my thoughts are not your thoughts, neither are your ways my ways," declares the Lord. *"As the heavens are higher than the earth, so are my ways higher than your ways and my thoughts than your thoughts."*
~ Isaiah 55:8–9

Blotches of algae marred the calm, dark lake. Sunlight twinkled on tiny waves. Occasionally, a fish splashed and disappeared. An egret flew just above the water.

A swimming anhinga stopped, waited a moment, ducked his long, thin neck into the water, and submerged. Even though I didn't see him, I knew that eventually he would emerge.

Anhingas, or snakebirds, were created to fish underwater. They have no oil on their feathers, like most birds. Therefore, they perch with wings spread out like large fans so they can dry.

The glassy lake showed no turmoil until a fish jumped and caused tiny waves. Although I could not see through the dark water, an unseen world of activity abounded.

A variety of water plants grow from the bottom to feed and hide wildlife. Fish swim and only occasionally break the surface of the lake. Snakes, frogs, and turtles live in two worlds, both above and below the water. Just because the underwater life isn't visible doesn't mean it doesn't exist. When I look around, evidence of thriving but concealed life abounds.

During our hardships, it is easy to believe God is not working and doesn't care about us because we see little proof in the natural. Then like the jumping fish, a glimmer of hope surfaces.

Often, by looking back, we see the miraculous ways he worked behind the scenes to protect and strengthen us for our journey.

Father, because we can't see you, we often miss what you are doing. But when we look carefully, there is evidence all around. Many times you use our adversities to produce something beautiful.
Amen.

DAY 41: LIMP AND LIFELESS

Therefore, I urge you, brothers and sisters, in view of God's mercy, to offer your bodies as a living sacrifice, holy and pleasing to God—this is your true and proper worship. Do not conform to the pattern of this world, but be transformed by the renewing of your mind. Then you will be able to test and approve what God's will is —his good, pleasing and perfect will.
~Romans 12:1–2

At the beginning of our shelter-at-home order in early spring, cool temperatures and low humidity greeted me for my daily walks and bike rides. By 8:00 a.m., I would be on my way and enjoyed meeting people around the neighborhood.

The government shutdown continued into late spring and summer, and conditions changed. I left my house earlier to escape the intense heat and high humidity. Few people ventured out at dawn, so I frequently had the streets and sidewalks to myself.

On my excursions, I dropped off pages from my daily devotionals at friends' homes. A few widows, who had recently lost their husbands, were regulars on my route. On special holidays like Mother's Day and Easter, my outreach grew to include more acquaintances and even some neighbors I didn't really know.

As I read my devotionals each morning, it was often easy to know who would benefit from each one. On other days, I prayed for the best message for each friend and left it up to God. People regularly told me that the messages were just what they needed for that day.

During the heat and high humidity of summer, I left home with crisp papers in my hand. At the first couple of stops, the pages remained firm and dry. Minutes later, my hand clutched limp, damp sheets that looked like they had been left in the rain.

Likewise, many lives during the pandemic became limp and lifeless. Solitude, uncertainty, and the loss of loved ones sapped people's energy and decreased their motivation.

Even though isolation kept me home month after month, I didn't want to become lethargic. My daily deliveries of uplifting devotional readings encouraged friends and energized me to continue sharing about Jesus.

Lord, don't let us get overtaken by the world, but transform us by renewing our minds as we share about Jesus.
Amen.

DAY 42: LESSONS FROM SOLITUDE

*You will keep the peace, a perfect peace,
for all who trust in You,
for those who dedicate
their hearts* and minds *to You.*
~ Isaiah 26:3 VOICE

Months and months of isolation during the pandemic gave me plenty of time for my daily devotionals. Early each day, I sat on my patio overlooking the lake and waited for a brilliant sunrise as I read and prayed.

However, at times, heavy clouds blocked the sun entirely. Other days, the yellow ball rose into a cloudless sky. Neither produced the hoped-for display.

One day, shades of pink swept across the eastern sky. With just the right amount of light and clouds, a spectacular presentation proclaimed the arrival of a new day. Birds circling the lake added their own chorus to the extravaganza. The long-awaited masterpiece filled me with joy as I absorbed the beauty before me.

I began singing, "I need Thee, oh, I need Thee. Every hour I need Thee…" The familiar but long forgotten hymn rose up from my memory to accompany God's lovely gift.

Within minutes, everything changed. Gray clouds wiped away the gorgeous spectacle like a gigantic eraser. A woodpecker's drilling blocked the sweet melodies. Gloom overtook it all.

Likewise during the pandemic, lives changed instantly. The virus disrupted the entire world. Death and illness swept from country to country. Robust economies screeched to a halt. Isolation separated communities and held people hostage. Fear and anxiety replaced happiness and contentment.

Even so, in my solitude, I learned important lessons. I found we can take time to be still and enjoy God's creation. There was more time to spend with Jesus and the Bible. We can show love to others and cherish our relationships.

Don't take blessings for granted. No one knows what tomorrow—or even today—will bring.

Loving Father, when we dedicate our hearts and minds to you,
we receive peace and contentment.
Help me trust you each day.
Amen.

DAY 43: BIBLE STUDY PARTY

Train up a child in the way he should go,
And when he is old
he will not depart from it.
~ Proverbs 22:6 NKJV

"Grandma, what's the name of your Bible study group?" Molly asked me.

"We don't have a name," I said.

Ten-year-old Molly informed me that we needed a name, so we selected "Bible Buddies" from her list of choices. Emily, her sister who normally doesn't work in the kitchen, decided to bake a cake for my group. She picked a strawberry mix, her grandpa's favorite and also the one she and her sisters enjoy.

When I peeked into my office, I saw craft items scattered on the desk.

Molly had made a colorful centerpiece from construction paper. She designed a "Bible Buddies" blue sign on my computer to attach to the front door. "Grandma, would you write down the names of the ladies who are coming?"

I did, and in a few minutes, she had made a personalized placemat on the computer for each woman.

Next, she made beautiful pendant necklaces for all of us with Scriptures written on them. She wanted a specific one for every person, so we picked out the verses together, then she wrote them on the paper pendants. She knew the best one for me would be Alan's favorite verse, Joshua 1:9: "Have I not commanded you? Be strong and courageous. Do not be afraid; do not be discouraged, for the LORD your God will be with you wherever you go."

While Emily baked the cake, Molly set the table with the personalized placemats, necklaces, and napkins. "Do we have a fancy plate for the cake?" she asked.

I pulled out my mother's cut-glass cake stand. The girls' eyes lit up when they saw it. Smiling, I brought out the matching glasses.

Emily carefully cut the cake and arranged it on the stand. My mom had used the cake stand for special occasions and would have loved having the girls continue her tradition.

"Don't cut the pieces too big," I said. "My friends don't eat a lot of sweets."

A little voice spoke up. "I thought old people ate a lot."

"Molly, you shouldn't say that," Emily told her.

Emily and I made eye contact and started laughing.

When my friends arrived, the sign, table arrangements, and gifts delighted them. The girls beamed. We all enjoyed the treats before our study began.

I loved seeing my granddaughters and friends come together for fellowship. And what a joy to see the fruit of serving in Emily's and Molly's lives as they blessed all of us.

Father, thank you for bringing generations together as we teach the younger ones to serve.
Amen.

DAY 44: DESTRUCTIVE WEEDS

Why, my soul, are you downcast?
Why so disturbed within me?
Put your hope in God,
for I will yet praise him,
my Savior and my God.
~ Psalm 42:5

Suffocating heat had kept me from yard work for weeks. A multitude of weeds popped up in flowerbeds and formed a green blanket over the mulch.

On my hands and knees, I began pulling up the invasive growth just as the sun rose. Wet grass drenched my pants. A light breeze tickled my sweaty brow. I looked at the daunting weeds. As I yanked out the offenders, a sense of accomplishment inspired me to keep going.

One type of invader came out easily and wasn't too large. A fan-shaped weed covered a large space, and when jerked from the center, it came out in one piece.

The worst intruder sent tall stems high and intertwined with my flowers. The roots branched out in long networks.

A small piece left behind would grow into more dominating and sprawling plants. Only by digging deep with a large shovel could I remove the entire thing, root and all.

In life, especially during periods of solitude, weeds of discontent, loneliness, and uncertainty grow and take root. A few can be extracted rather easily, but others are more deep-rooted and destructive.

I have learned to focus more on Jesus. Reading the Bible gives me peace and strength for whatever comes. I am more content and less anxious.

Scriptures remind me that this is not our home and that, as Christians, we are ambassadors for God.

Being grateful brings joy, peace, and contentment.

Jehovah, when we are lonely and downcast, give us hope in you.
Fill us with praise and thankfulness.
Amen.

DAY 45: PREDICTED OR UNPREDICTED STORMS

"And do not seek what you should eat or what you should drink, nor have an anxious mind. For all these things the nations of the world seek after, and your Father knows that you need these things. But seek the kingdom of God, and all these things shall be added to you."
~ *Luke 12:29–32 NKJV*

Constant, frantic alerts filled the airwaves. Weather maps with colorful, spaghetti lines showed the approaching hurricane's possible paths. For several days, the relentless forecasts dominated the news.

News reports admonished everyone to prepare for the hurricane by purchasing batteries, water, medications, and food. Fill cars with gas. After a while, my mind blocked their incessant warnings.

Even though the hype continued, the storm-watch forecasters admitted that wind speeds dropped. The projected horrible tempest was no longer even a hurricane—it was downgraded to a tropical storm. However, many people, especially new residents and visitors, panicked at the potential devastation that might happen.

Instead of being afraid, I turned off the television and went about my normal activities. The predicted storm only brought a little rain our way.

A few days later, summer thunderstorms resumed in our area with a vengeance. With little warning, a heavy rainstorm hit. Rain swept across my patio. Trees whipped wildly in the gusts. Hail beat against my windows and battered my plants. Dark clouds brought evening early.

I searched for damage by looking out one window after another as the ferocious gales lashed my house. Then I gathered candles, matches, and a flashlight in case the electricity went off.

Afternoon thunderstorms rocked the area for days. Those normal summer storms produced more rain, wind, and hail than the much-publicized possible hurricane. That anticipated storm caused worry and anxiety for so many but no catastrophe for my area.

Often, we fear tragedies that never occur. Then we can be hit with unexpected adversities that are on a smaller scale but nonetheless devastating. Being prepared for emergencies is advantageous whether they are large or small.

But trusting God can eliminate panic and desperation. He stilled the squall on the Sea of Galilee with just a word, and he can calm our storms too.

Loving Father, still our minds and hearts. Help us seek you instead of worrying about possible storms.
Amen.

DAY 46: A SPARKLE IN THE MESS

*Now may the God of hope fill you with all joy and
peace as you trust in him,
that you may overflow with hope
by the power of the Holy Spirit.
~ Romans 15:13*

Every year, steamy summer weather hits Florida. For months, forecasters can use the same daily forecast: temperatures in the nineties, high humidity, and possible rain.

Floridians adapt to the extreme heat and humidity by going outside early in the day or later in the evening. We rush from our homes to the car and then into cool, air-conditioned buildings, enduring the relentless summers knowing we avoid frigid temperatures, blizzards, and extended periods of sunless days.

However, the heat often brings more unwanted effects. When I looked at my lake, clumps of ugly algae dotted the surface. Swirls of disgusting green masses coated sections of the water.

Normally, I enjoy changes in my lake. At dawn and sunset it regularly looks like a mirror. Breezes bring ripples, and gales turn it into raging waves. I love watching the different stages, but not the recent ugliness.

The fluttering of the wind disturbed the murkiness. A tiny sparkle of clear water pierced the darkness.

Similarly, during the plight of the pandemic, beacons of light glowed. At a doctor's appointment, the receptionist said, "There is no charge for today because of COVID."

At Publix, people weren't as frightened to speak to each other as we were at the beginning of the shutdown. A clerk, a bagger, and I talked about the charity I was buying items for.

Neighbors chatted with old friends and made new ones on walks around the neighborhood.

Even in our trying times, we can appreciate the sparkle from the lights of hope that occasionally appear in the midst of chaos.

Loving Father, we struggle as we deal with so many problems. Fill us with joy, peace, and hope in the middle of our uncertain world.
Amen.

DAY 47: HUMMINGBIRDS, BEES, AND BUTTERFLIES

The LORD is my strength and my shield; my heart trusts in him, and he helps me. My heart leaps for joy, and with my song I praise him.
~ Psalm 28:7

Spires of flowering plants lined the back of my patio. Bell-shaped blooms of crimson, orange, and white decorated green stems. Both kinds of flowers came from the clearance rack at Lowe's.

A couple of years ago, I dug holes and dropped the withered plants into the ground. With plenty of water and sunshine, they flourished. Occasionally, I trimmed dead leaves and out-of-bounds foliage, but mostly I let them grow on their own.

Tiny plants grew to be over four feet tall and formed a lovely addition to my garden. They attracted a variety of winged creatures. Monarch butterflies swooped down for a visit. Fuzzy bumblebees zoomed from one flower to another. They grabbed onto the blossoms and stuck their heads into white and red-orange petals almost every day.

Although I enjoyed watching all the visitors, hummingbirds were my favorite. Whirling wings allowed them to hover as their slender beaks dipped into the red-orange flowers for delectable treats. I wondered why they always bypassed the white ones.

Some days they drank briefly and disappeared. At other times, the pair of teeny birds hung in the air as if by magic above one plant and another before drinking the nectar from the flower cups. Then they whizzed away.

At our previous home, Alan put up a hummingbird feeder that he meticulously cleaned and filled with hummingbird food. Because it was away from the house, we didn't see many birds visit. After we moved, the bird feeder remained in the garage, and when Alan passed away, I didn't want another thing to take care of so I gave the red feeder away.

In my isolation, I found more time to appreciate nature. I had no idea my clearance-rack plants would bring such joy to my garden. Hummingbirds came more frequently, or perhaps I noticed them because I had slowed down.

In addition to my increasing gratitude for my retreat on the lake, cherished family and friends have become even more precious. As life becomes more normal, I don't want my busyness to overshadow a heartfelt thankfulness for God's gifts.

Heavenly Father, thank you for the world you made.
Help us rejoice in it daily.
Amen.

DAY 48: TOPPLED BUSH

*"For I, the L*ORD *your God,*
will hold your right hand,
Saying to you, 'Fear not, I will help you.'"
~ Isaiah 41:13 NKJV

Wind battered the cypress and oak trees in my yard. Limbs thrashed in every direction during the raging summer storm. Bits of hail hit my windows. Thunder and lightning produced a frightening fireworks display as I watched the power of the storm.

Eventually, weary limbs stilled. Thunder rumbled in the distance. Only then did I venture outside to check for damage.

The furious downpour had crippled a rescued bush that had strong branches and plentiful yellow blooms until the thunderstorm hit. The rain-soaked ground loosened the sturdy trunk and tipped the healthy plant almost to the ground. A decision had to be made about the unsightly shrub before it fell over completely.

First, I cut heavy branches off as I tried to decide its fate. Before I could put the trimmings in a garbage bag, the bees returned. They stuck furry heads into smiling blooms and collected nectar from the clippings on the ground. I stopped working and watched the busy insects work.

Pruning didn't fix the unsteady bush, but I couldn't face digging up the once-beautiful blossoming plant. It needed a second chance.

With two short wooden poles from my garage jammed into the ground, I struggled to enclose the errant limbs with yellow tape. I pulled with all my strength, and the bush stood as tall as I did. Knots held. I hoped it would withstand the next storm.

Day after day, the roots had a chance to push deeper and hold steady. Bees visited daily. Yellow blooms made me smile. Although it leaned slightly, the wooden stakes gave the needed reinforcement to the crooked bush.

Months of multiple disasters caused uneasiness, anger, and depression for many people. Difficult circumstances extinguished hope and brought despair. Like the small pegs, support from loved ones, encouraging phone calls, and thoughtful texts increased our limited strength to help prop us up temporarily.

But lasting strength, peace, and comfort come only from God.

Father, your whispers of encouragement reduce our anxiety. Thank you for holding us up.
Amen.

DAY 49: MOUNTAINS WE CLIMB

I lift up my eyes to the mountains—
where does my help come from?
*My help comes from the L*ORD*,*
the Maker of heaven and earth.
He will not let your foot slip—
he who watches over you will not slumber;
indeed, he who watches over Israel
will neither slumber nor sleep.
~ Psalm 121:1–4

In my dark bedroom, sparks of illumination blazed through my shutters like someone switching a light off and on. No thunder roared, but the flares of light continued.

When I settled down in my favorite chair on the patio a while later, lightning flashed around me. Dark clouds circled the lake. A blue and pink sky loomed above the gray peaks.

The scene reminded me of mountainous views in Colorado, North Carolina, Switzerland, and other precipitous regions around the world. The vast and powerful sky, like the mountain ranges, showcased the majesty and beauty of God's creation.

Climbing these steep cliffs brings perils and danger, but rewards as well. Although we're perhaps battered and beaten during the ascent, a prize awaits at the peak with stunning views and a profound sense of accomplishment.

The large cumulus clouds, though different from their rocky counterparts, can also bring splendor and challenges. Many people face their own mountains, especially when living alone. My circle of widow friends continues to grow. Together, we have faced grief, loneliness, and, for some, even despair. Separation from the world brings additional challenges for those who are single through the loss of a spouse.

Battles with cancer, heart disease, divorce, financial concerns, job loss, and other trials can seem like insurmountable heights for people around the world. However, the pink-and-blue sky signaled hope, joy, and encouragement for me. The brilliantly colored heavens gave me an assurance of a way out of my isolation and confirmation that we are not alone in our struggles.

Relying on Jesus each day has inspired me to continue to the peak of my highlands. When the next one appears, I can look back upon the trek I've already made and know I can scale the next one since God is still my guide.

God, when we rely on you, we climb our mountains
with joy and finish with peace.
Amen.

DAY 50: TIME AT THE LAB

Let the words of my mouth and the meditation of my heart
Be acceptable in Your sight,
*O L*ORD*, my strength and my Redeemer.*
~ Psalm 19:14 NKJV

A line of masked people stood like perfectly distanced soldiers as we waited for lab work. Each time a temperature was taken, the line moved up six feet. A few entered the building, but most returned to their cars to wait on a call to come inside for testing.

The man behind me voiced a slew of grievances about the need for masks, the wait, the process, and the state of the world.

We inched forward. The lady checking us in said she normally worked in an office. Her eyes above her face covering expressed discontent as she endured endless complaints.

I finally entered the air-conditioned facility. Around the room, masks hid scowls and brows furrowed in annoyance and frustration. Two people, who had been first in line but didn't have a cell phone, waited while others had blood drawn and left.

A worker pointed me to a cubicle where patients normally checked in. "Your call didn't go through, so you have to answer some questions on that phone."

Obediently, I sat at the desk with plexiglass behind the phone and a bottle of hand sanitizer next to me. Because I was alone, I took down my face covering.

The healthcare worker noticed. "You have to put that on!"

"I have asthma and have trouble breathing with a mask."

"I understand," she said. But her voice and mannerisms lacked compassion.

I pushed the mask back up on my face. The whole craziness of the situation made me sad. Kind people who were thrust into exasperating situations became short-tempered. I tried to remember they were only following instructions.

Eventually, my name was called. The technician cheerfully took my blood. Normally, I make conversation, but not on that day. I only briefly answered her questions.

The virus caused disruptions and undue fear. Irritations overcame kindness. Absurd regulations replaced common sense. A web of uncertainty and fear entangled all of us.

My foul mood followed me home and then to a luncheon. When a lady at my table revealed her serious health conditions, the icy shell around my heart melted. Even though I hadn't voiced my frustrations to the workers at the lab, I grumbled to other patients. God knew the condition of my heart and humbled me with my friend's grave problems.

We need to watch our words and protect our hearts as we continue to deal with difficult situations.

Loving Father, thank you for loving us when we are unlovable.
Help our words and hearts be acceptable to you.
Amen.

DAY 51: VISITING CARDINALS

*Search me, O God, and know my heart; try me and know my
anxieties; And see if there is any wicked way
in me, and lead me in the way everlasting.*
~ Psalm 139:23–24 NKJV

Anxiety crept into my bed and stole sleep. Disturbing news stories and conversations with friends distressed about the condition of our world added fear and uncertainty. Praying and trying to ignore the turmoil didn't work. Tragic situations that friends were experiencing added weight and squeezed hope from my heart.

Instead of praying to God, I took on the problems of my friends and the horrors of the world. No matter how many times the troubles swirled in my head and disturbed my sleep, no resolutions came from my little brain. Worry brought no solutions, but kept me from listening for God's answers.

Before dawn, I shuffled outside with my cup of tea. A spot of lamplight shined on my books. One reading after another spoke of peace, gratitude, and trust in Jesus. As my focus turned to my Savior, anxiety started to float away.

In my special haven, a vibrant sunrise replaced darkness and covered the sky. Dew-drenched blooms bordered my patio and sparkled in sunlight. Songbirds welcomed the dawn with delightful melodies.

A pair of cardinals perched among yellow flowers a few feet from me. Their beaks nipped at leaves as they tweeted to each other and then flew away. God adorned them in lovely feathers and provided just what they needed.

My serene retreat refreshed me as I pushed the disturbing world away and enjoyed nature around me. In the distance, I heard humming traffic on the highway but could not see it. Nor did I allow it to join me in my sanctuary.

This day I was especially thankful for my daily devotional time that fortifies me before I venture out and helps me avoid the pitfalls of negativity. God's love, wisdom, and peace protect and encircle me. He provides armor for whatever the world slams at me.

If God cares for the cardinals, how much more does he care for you and me.

Loving Father, search us and know our anxieties. Guide and protect us as we venture into the world.
Amen.

DAY 52: CREATURES IN THE DARK

But let all who take refuge in you be glad;
let them ever sing for joy.
Spread your protection over them,
that those who love your name may rejoice in you.
*Surely, L*ORD*, you bless the righteous;*
you surround them with your favor as a shield.
~ Psalm 5:11–12

A single light bulb illuminated my Bible and devotional books. Darkness wrapped my patio like an ebony cocoon. Eerie noises, like screeching voices, interrupted my meditation. My eyes searched the shadows for the culprits but saw nothing.

In my mind, possible hidden dangers lurked beyond the patio screen. The unusual commotion created images in my mind of dragons and menacing obstacles that could overtake me.

But as beams of light broke through the blackness, dawn revealed serenity. No ferocious creatures emerged from the forest or the lake. Instead of mysterious piercing squeals, birds sang harmonious, soothing songs.

In our chaotic world, constant voices shriek and bellow their agendas to cause terror and distress. Truth or lies about the upheaval in the world, including riots, injustice, job loss, politicians, health care, etc. permeate the airwaves. Dangers lurk. Invisible beasts destroy order and harmony.

Answers won't come from the government, politicians, the media, or a friend's post on Facebook.

God is the answer. He removes panic and worry from our hearts and minds. He gives contentment and joy in the midst of uncertainty and turbulence. His love endures forever.

Loving Father, calm our hearts with your wisdom, faithfulness, and compassion. You are our refuge and shield.
Replace our fearfulness with your serenity.
Amen.

DAY 53: KINDNESS AT WALMART

Beloved, if God so loved us, we also ought to love one another.
~ *1 John 4:11 NKJV*

On my way home from church, I drove up and down the parking lot aisles at Walmart to find an empty spot. Finally, far from the entrance, I left my car and walked into the crowded store.

Near the front doors, a young lady half-heartedly sprayed the shopping carts with disinfectant. She gave a couple of squirts on the inside of the carts but nothing on the handles.

My cloth shopping bag protected my hands when I placed it on the unsanitized cart handle and maneuvered through the crowded, narrow aisles. A few items went into the metal basket as I roamed from one section to another.

In the unfamiliar store, I had no idea where to find Scotch Guard for my new porch cushions. A worker stocking shelves searched her device to find the correct area and pointed to the back.

From one department to another, I searched for the illusive Scotch Guard. A man in a Walmart shirt noticed my consternation and asked if he could help. He had no success either. But he led me to the section for the motion lights that I also needed. Though our time together was brief, his cheerful attitude warmed my heart.

"Thank you," I said.

"God bless you," he replied after he directed me toward the cleaning supplies. He instantly disappeared to assist another customer.

Across the huge store, I located the cleaning supplies. Another friendly worker looked for Scotch Guard. Neither of us found the missing product either. "As soon as products come in, they are gone," he said and pointed to the empty shelves.

"I guess people are home and have more time to clean."

He responded, "They should have been cleaning anyway."

We laughed. Even in difficult circumstances, I met three friendly workers who graciously assisted me. Their attitudes made my heart happy even though I didn't find everything I had hoped to buy.

Even during turmoil, we can be kind and caring.

Lord, thank you for those who are kind even when their circumstances might be difficult too.
Remind us to love others.
Amen.

DAY 54: TURBULENT TIMES

God is our refuge and strength, an ever-present help in trouble. Therefore we will not fear, though the earth give way and the mountains fall into the heart of the sea, though its waters roar and foam and the mountains quake with their surging.
There is a river whose streams make glad the city of God, the holy place where the Most High dwells. God is within her, she will not fall; God will help her at break of day.
Nations are in uproar, kingdoms fall; he lifts his voice, the earth melts. The LORD Almighty is with us;
the God of Jacob is our fortress.
~ Psalm 46:1–7

A never-ending barrage of angry waves crashed against the beach. Ominous clouds blocked the sun. Only a few brave souls ventured into the intense winds as high tide pushed water farther and farther up the sand.

During the evening, waves calmed. The ocean receded and exposed more of the beach. Clumps of brown seaweed littered the white sand. I shook my head at the blight on the normally pristine seashore. To avoid the ugly mess, I zigzagged through the clutter during my evening walk.

At the beginning of my vacation, the beauty of the white sand beach stretched endlessly. The following day, turbulent winds churned the water, pulled up unsightly seaweed, and spit it out as refuse. After the storm, I hoped the tides would retrieve the rubbish and return it to the ocean.

Down the coastline, hundreds of sandpipers tiptoed along the ocean. A few courageous birds scampered to the seaweed and stuck long beaks into the ugly masses for morsels of food. The birds weren't afraid of the dreadful, smelly eyesores and instead discovered benefits and sustenance from them.

Our world spits out one mess after another. We can lament over the shambles left behind or trust God and look for blessings within them.

Loving Father, you give us strength even when our world is shaken. Help us be still and trust you to show us the blessings in the midst of the messes.
Amen.

DAY 55: DANGER BENEATH THE SURFACE

*Place your trust in the Eternal; rely on Him completely; never depend upon your own ideas and inventions. Give Him the credit for everything you accomplish, and He will smooth out and straighten the road that lies ahead.
And don't think you can decide on your own what is right and what is wrong. Respect the Eternal; turn and run from evil.*
~ *Proverbs 3:5–7 VOICE*

Cars whizzed across the expressway over Lake Jessup, one of the largest bodies of water in Florida. Sunlight lit up tiny waves on the expansive lake like twinkling Christmas lights. The clear, blue sky and enchanting lake made me smile but also reminded me of the dangers.

Occasionally, a fisherman threw out a line or a boater ventured onto the water. But swimmers and skiers avoided it unless they were newcomers to the area. The reality of what lies beneath the sparkling surface is a serious threat. The once-pristine gem is no longer. Years ago, nuisance gators were released into the giant lake. Now, almost thirteen thousand alligators are estimated to live there.

Runoff from around the lake sent pollutants into the water. The highway built across the lake added berms and pillars that disturbed the natural flow of water that used to clean the lake. This combination of factors created a mostly unusable body of water for humans to enjoy even though it still looks appealing.

Life is also filled with enticing people, places, and activities that appear trustworthy, decent, and suitable. However, below the surface, perils await. Often, it is difficult to see the camouflaged risks.

In our unsettling times, danger, deceit, and lies surround us. We must be on guard and pray for wisdom and direction each day in both small and big situations.

*Lord, help us learn to trust you in all we do as we
listen and follow your instructions. Give us wisdom as
we run to you and flee from evil.*
Amen.

DAY 56: STABS OF PAIN

*Do you take the kindness of God for granted?
Do you see His patience and tolerance as signs that
He is a pushover when it comes to sin?
How could you not know that His kindness is guiding
our hearts to turn away from distractions and
habitual sin to walk a new path?*
~ Romans 2:4 VOICE

Light poked through the trees as dawn awoke my small lake. Hidden birds sang their morning tunes. A great blue heron stood on the shore and waited for breakfast. The sky turned from gray to pink.

With my Bible, devotional books, and journals, I settled down in my wicker chair on the patio. I began writing in my gratitude journal, and a minor prick of pain distracted me. I stopped writing to examine my leg but saw nothing unusual.

As I began reading a devotional, a second twinge startled me and disrupted my concentration. Once again, I looked up and down my leg to find the source of the irritation with no success.

Even though I began reading the Bible, my mind wandered from the words to my stinging leg. A needle-like jab stung me for the third time. With every stab, the aching intensified as did my determination to find the offender. Upon examination of my leg again, I noticed a tiny ant next to a red welt above my knee.

The teeny critter disrupted my time with God because of its minor but throbbing sting. Because of the irritant, I couldn't fully engage in my reading and praying. The effects of the bite diverted my attention even after I found the culprit.

Days later, the red spot remained as a painful reminder of often small or unseen but perilous distractions. Allowing diversions and hindrances to overtake our thoughts and attention robs us of God's blessings.

Loving Father, show us what is important and what is not.
Guide us in ignoring distractions and sins that
pull us away from your best for us.
Amen.

DAY 57: A THANKSGIVING IN SOLITUDE

Do not be anxious about anything, but in every situation, by
prayer and petition, with thanksgiving,
present your requests to God.
And the peace of God,
which transcends all understanding,
will guard your hearts and your minds in Christ Jesus.
~ Philippians 4:6–7

Hours before dawn, my eyes opened. Soon I remembered it was Thanksgiving Day and we were still in a pandemic. After tossing and turning for an hour, I threw back the covers and ventured into the blackness.

One tiny virus had brought such distress with deaths, illnesses, shutdowns, riots, and job losses. Each dreadful situation produced even more serious consequences. Everyone around the world was affected.

My mind replayed our previous Thanksgivings. Most were joyous celebrations with family members.

Now the disease assaulted even Thanksgiving. Many large celebrations were canceled and travel eliminated. Around the United States, smaller groups planned to assemble, but some families decided not to gather at all. For the first time ever, I wouldn't be with anyone in my family. When loneliness and sadness attacked, I thought of my blessings instead.

Friends invited me to join them for lunch outside at a local restaurant in the beautiful Florida sunshine. Later on, I prepared a traditional Thanksgiving meal of turkey, dressing, mashed potatoes, and cranberry salad for myself, and enjoyed several meals of leftovers. No one I knew had a normal Thanksgiving, but we all adapted.

Thanksgiving Day is a marvelous time to thank God for the gifts he has given us. However, we should be thankful constantly instead of only on one day.

As I think of God's blessings, the list is endless. Although I wasn't with my family, I connected by phone and on my computer. My screen filled with my children, grandchildren, great-grandchildren, cousins, and friends. I live in a lovely home on a peaceful lake. I am allowed to go to church when I want to and freely read my Bible. I live in a country of many freedoms. On this day and every day, I choose gratitude despite undesirable circumstances.

Loving Father, as the world goes through a season of constant trials, thank you for being with us. Nudge us to be thankful no matter our circumstances.
Amen.

DAY 58: AN ALPHABET OF THANKFULNESS

Rejoice always, pray continually, give thanks in all circumstances; for this is God's will for you in Christ Jesus.
~ *1 Thessalonians 5:16–18*

I read Paul's instructions as I looked out at another dreary day. No gorgeous sunrise or fluffy clouds. A series of text messages and emails told of crisis after crisis with family and friends. I muttered under my breath to no one, "Be thankful? Really?"

Every day I add entries to my gratitude journal, but after reading a chapter of Max Lucado's book *Before Amen: The Power of Simple Prayer*, I decided to try his approach of using the alphabet to produce a list of blessings.

A – apple a day keeps the doctor away
B – brothers who enriched my life
C – chocolate (dark) is good for the heart
D – dad who took care of me
E – elephants in the wild in Namibia on a mission trip
F – friends who support me
G – granddaughters who are loving and kind

H – heart that the cardiologist says is strong
I – internet that keeps me connected
J – job that provided purpose and income for many years
K – kitchen where I can cook
L – lawn that forms a carpet around my home
M – mother who nurtured and loved me
N – neighbors who are friendly and helpful
O – oranges for Vitamin C
P – patio where I sit and enjoy the lake
Q – quartet of gospel singers
R – relaxing time to be renewed
S – son who loves his family
T – tea every day
U – uniforms that signify those who help others
V – vases for all my flowers
W – wind that rustles trees
X – x-rays to help doctors diagnose
Y – yellow sunshine
Z – zebras that are an amazing part of creation

Once I started, it was easy to continue, and I looked forward to making my next list. Gratefulness makes each day brighter, even in difficult times.

Loving Father, thank you for our lives and all you have done for us. We have so much to be thankful for.
Amen.

DAY 59: THE PINK GIFT

*Every good and perfect gift is from above, coming
down from the Father of the heavenly lights, who does
not change like shifting shadows.*
~ James 1:17

A rosy glow covered the trees, grass, lake, and sky like a sheer scarf in a fanciful dream. Nothing looked real as I gazed at the lake behind my home. For several minutes, I enjoyed the rosy world around me and marveled at the unusual beauty. A sense of peace, joy, and expectation filled me like a balm even in the midst of an uncommon year.

But within a short time, the sun climbed higher and swept away the extraordinary phenomenon. Normalcy returned with green grass, a few lingering orange and white flowers, and trees changing from green to gold.

A white egret ascended from the shore and sailed above the lake. Four stately sandhill cranes strode across my yard. A pair of ducks formed a wake on the still water as they swam to the far shore.

Although I missed the spectacular colors from the sunrise, I enjoyed the beauty of my sunlit lake view too. Whether sunny, rainy, or cloudy, my special retreat gives me peace and contentment.

Frequently, we expect to see God in the spectacular, but he more frequently appears in the ordinary. A child's laugh and exuberance. A needed hug. A smile through tears. A special song. The smell of a favorite meal. A dependable car. Food in the refrigerator. Countless other blessings.

In the busyness of ordinary lives, it is easy to overlook God's gifts in the mundane.

> *Loving Father, what wonderful surprises you give to your children. Many times we are so busy that we overlook them and don't even open the gifts. Help us learn to look for you each day. As that becomes a habit, we will see you more clearly and appreciate your love for us.*
> *Amen.*

DAY 60: PLAY LIKE CHILDREN

Then they also brought infants to Him that He might touch them; but when the disciples saw it, they rebuked them. But Jesus called them to Him and said, "Let the little children come to Me, and do not forbid them; for of such is the kingdom of God. Assuredly, I say to you, whoever does not receive the kingdom of God as a little child will by no means enter it."
~ Luke 18:15–17 NKJV

"Grandma, can we go to the park and take Peyton?" Molly asked.

"Sure," I said.

A short time later, my ten-year-old granddaughter and her friend Peyton rode with me to a nearby park. The girls scrambled to the slide and played tag around the playground equipment while I sat on a nearby bench. As they romped, I enjoyed the bright sunshine and mild temperature.

When they tired of the playground, we walked across a field to a gigantic oak tree. Limbs towered high above us, while others stretched out like an octopus's tentacles just low enough for the girls to reach.

They walked on long limbs with arms outstretched like gymnasts. I watched from my perch on a low bough. As pretend fairies, they swirled and danced around the tree. At their request, I gave them fairy names.

When the pixies tired, the girls turned into pioneers and tried to start fires by rubbing dry sticks together. Each of them formed a small stone fire pit with moss and leaves in the center. Their patience waned when no sparks appeared.

They ran across a playing field to a large statue of a baseball glove. I caught up with them as they examined the sculpture. They then ran to a second playground. I followed at a leisurely pace.

During the afternoon, there was no mention of isolation, the economy, or any other troublesome world events. Molly and Peyton relished being together in the beautiful weather, and so did I.

As adults, we can become obsessed with current problems and possible future ones. Then we ignore the special people and places around us. Sometimes we should relax and enjoy life like children do. Swing high. Run in the park. Climb a tree. Laugh and pretend. Play and don't take life so seriously.

Loving Father, thank you for the spontaneity and joy of children. Help us enjoy life and accept your blessings even in hard times.
Amen.

DAY 61: WHERE IS BABY JESUS?

Now after Jesus was born in Bethlehem of Judea in the days of Herod the king, behold, wise men from the East came to Jerusalem, saying, "Where is He who has been born King of the Jews? For we have seen His star in the East and have come to worship Him."
~ Matthew 2:1–2 NKJV

When my three granddaughters came to help me decorate for Christmas, Emily displayed the nativity sets, Ashlyn worked on the tree, and Molly decorated the front door area.

Each year the entertainment center holds my collection of nativity sets from around the world, including ones I found on trips to Israel and Peru. It is a perfect place to showcase the scenes so I can look at them every day.

"Grandma, I can't find baby Jesus," Emily said.

Most of the nativities had already been set up when Emily gave her disturbing announcement. I joined her to look for the missing baby Jesus from the set Alan bought in Kenya.

I picked up the papers that had wrapped each piece of the carved white stone figures. No baby Jesus. Puzzled at his disappearance, we knew we couldn't display the nativity without Jesus.

Emily held up a large, white cherub from my angel collection. "We can use this for when the Wise Men arrived."

We laughed. We knew Jesus had grown by the time the Wise Men appeared, but the angel still wouldn't work.

Then I glanced at the shelf. "There is baby Jesus."

Emily couldn't believe it. She had placed the baby beside the lambs. "I thought that was another sheep," she said.

All of us laughed at her confusion. That set always gave me trouble too because the stone images didn't look like traditional figures. Sometimes, I couldn't discern the shepherds from the Wise Men or even Joseph. Although I had never mistaken the Jesus sculpture for a sheep, he is the Lamb of God. We decided it made sense.

When life doesn't go the way we think it should, we may assume Jesus doesn't care and has deserted us. He hasn't gotten lost, but sometimes we do.

Father, thank you for reminding us that Jesus isn't lost. Just as the Wise Men looked for him, we often search for him too. He continues to work in our lives, but we need to be open to seeing Him.
Amen.

DAY 62: NO ROOM

Therefore the Lord himself will give you a sign: the virgin will conceive and give birth to a son, and will call him Immanuel.
~ *Isaiah 7:14*

Every bump in the road and sway of the donkey jostled Mary. The treacherous journey would have been hard for anyone, but especially for a very pregnant teenager. Finally, the twinkling lights of Bethlehem beckoned the exhausted couple.

"I will find a warm place for you to rest, Mary," her husband, Joseph, said before he went to look for lodging.

Her aching body longed for a warm, soft bed. Her stomach growled. She waited for Joseph to return from the inn.

"No room," he said. Although the narrow streets were crowded, he knew a place would soon be found.

At the second stop, no vacancy as well. Mary nodded and hoped the next inn would accommodate them.

Joseph trudged into another crowded guesthouse. "Sorry, no room," the innkeeper said. When he saw Joseph's dejected face, he continued, "There is a small cave in back where animals stay. You would be out of the cold."

Joseph attempted a smile when he returned to Mary. "There is no room at the inn, but the innkeeper is allowing us to stay in a cave with his animals."

With no other choice, Mary agreed. Joseph guided her into the dim, smelly stable. Cattle mooed. Sheep rustled.

The doting husband threw a cloak on the floor and helped Mary settle down. Despite her labor pain, she smiled. "Thank you, Joseph."

After hearing messages from the angels and realizing it wouldn't be easy, they had each accepted the vast calling on their life. Mary's out-of-wedlock pregnancy had shocked the community, and Joseph's reaction in support of his soon-to-be wife brought more questions.

Because Mary carried the Son of God, the couple believed God would provide for them. But they discovered one obstacle after another. Isolated, tired, and rejected, they settled in among the animals and straw. They wondered at the circumstances and waited.

Like Mary and Joseph, we wait as we long for an end to our isolation. We look ahead with expectancy to see how God will work and still feel despair with all the tragedies and imagine more disasters to come.

During Advent, like Mary and Joseph, we anticipate the coming of Jesus. Problems should not overtake our joy and peace, now or in the future.

Caring Father, thank you for providing for us even in hard times and when we are tired of waiting.
Amen.

DAY 63: HEAVENLY MESSENGERS

*Now there were in the same country shepherds living out in the
fields, keeping watch over their flock by night.
And behold, an angel of the Lord stood before them, and the glory
of the Lord shone around them, and they were greatly afraid.
Then the angel said to them,
"Do not be afraid, for behold, I bring you good tidings of great
joy which will be to all people. For there is
born to you this day in the city of David
a Savior, who is Christ the Lord."
~ Luke 2:8–11 NKJV*

An exhausted Mary tossed and turned to ease her pain. Nothing helped. Soon the inexperienced couple delivered the precious baby. Mary wrapped Jesus in swaddling clothes.

Joseph placed clean hay in a stone feeding trough, a crude crib for the King. As the new mother placed the baby in his bed, voices interrupted the tranquility and isolation.

Firelight illuminated expectant faces that stared from the mouth of the cave.

One man said, "We were on the hills outside of the village watching our sheep. All at once, we heard a voice from above that terrified us. We fell to the ground as light filled the sky."

Another shepherd added, "An angel told us not to be afraid. He said we should be joyful."

"We tried to understand the wondrous news. A chorus of angels sang, 'Glory to God in the highest, and on earth peace, goodwill toward men.' We followed the heavenly instructions and hurried into Bethlehem to find this baby who will save us."

Unlikely messengers followed the star to Jesus. They obeyed, praised God, and repeated the Good News about baby Jesus.

As we look for Jesus in our unsettled world, we must be open to his message even when delivered by unlikely messengers. If God used despised, dirty shepherds to announce Jesus's birth, our Lord can surprise the world now too. Perhaps even use us to spread his message of hope.

Father, thank you for the wonderful gift of Jesus that brings us joy. Help us listen to your messengers and also deliver the gospel to the world.
Amen.

DAY 64: THE CHRISTMAS STAR

*When they saw the star,
they rejoiced with
exceedingly great joy.
~ Matthew 2:10 NKJV*

At dusk, I drove through my community to find a clear view of the sky. Near a small lake, cars lined the street, so I turned around to see if they were also looking for the Christmas star.

Clusters of people stood around two telescopes. Friends talked. Many of us were strangers who stopped to watch the much-publicized phenomenon.

We all searched the darkening sky for the bright star. With a sky app that showed planets and constellations, one man pointed us in the right direction, where planes crisscrossed through the clouds.

The crowd stared at two tiny dots of light through binoculars, telescopes, and with the naked eye. More bystanders watched the occurrence with phone apps and shared the pictures with neighbors.

Because of the news reports of a grand spectacle, most of us expected a brilliant show. But clouds drifted across a pair of teeny white dots.

One woman said, "How did the Wise Men follow *that?*"

A few people returned to their cars. The rest of us continued to watch and hoped the star would grow brighter, but it didn't.

Later, in my own yard, I gazed at the underwhelming small lights faraway. Alone, I imagined the shepherds also in the dark on the first Christmas Eve. They must have been astonished to see angels appear and interrupt their quiet night with a magnificent, heavenly display that filled the night sky.

As Christmas approached, people around the world anticipated joy, peace, and an end to the virus that had interrupted our lives. A breathtaking Christmas star would have increased our hope for a more normal holiday. But the star didn't live up to our expectations.

We desired drastic, miraculous changes and an end to tribulation. Sometimes God works that way. But God often arrives in unlikely circumstances to ordinary people like Mary, Joseph, and the shepherds, as he did when Jesus was born on that starry night in a stable with animals in Bethlehem.

During Advent, Christians anticipate and celebrate the arrival of Jesus. We can open our hearts and minds to his presence in unexpected ways even when we don't get what we hope for.

Don't overlook the important while searching for the stupendous. He is a God of surprises.

Emmanuel, help us see you in both big and small ways. Fill us with joy even when our expectations are not met.
Amen.

DAY 65: LIFE IN DESPAIR

Teacher: For everything that happens in life—there is a season, a
right time for everything under heaven:
A time to be born, a time to die;
a time to plant, a time to collect the harvest;
A time to kill, a time to heal; a time to tear down,
a time to build up;
A time to cry, a time to laugh; a time to mourn, a time to dance;...
I have seen the kinds of tasks God has given each of us to do to
keep one busy, and I know God has made everything beautiful for
its time. God has also placed in our minds a sense of eternity; we
look back on the past and ponder over the future, yet we cannot
understand the doings of God.
~ Ecclesiastes 3:1–4, 10–11 VOICE

Sunlight sparkled on intricate spider webs. Water droplets on the screen shimmered like tiny diamonds.

On the cypress trees by the lake, a few rust-colored needles hung onto branches like a scraggly coat. Touches of gray Spanish moss swayed in the breeze like a frayed scarf. Fatigue and discouragement emanated from the almost-barren trees.

But as I continued to stare at the forlorn forest, I noticed a squirrel at the end of a nearly naked branch. He grabbed a tuft of dead needles and scampered to the top of the tree. I loved that he ignored the bleakness around him, found a hidden treasure, and scurried away to enjoy it.

My view of the wretched cypress trees reminded me of the effects of the pandemic. One catastrophe followed by another filled all our minds and hearts around the world. Month after month brought more sadness and despair. It seemed bad news never stopped. Although we continued to face countless difficult situations and had no idea when it would end, there were moments of happiness.

Like the little squirrel, we can find peace and joy even in the bleakness of isolation, shutdowns, and illnesses. For example, watching wildlife, laughing with a child, or visiting with friends on a Zoom call can change our focus from pain to pleasure. Depression turns to joy even in adversity.

Loving Father, we don't understand why we have so many struggles with no apparent end. We do know that you are still in control through each season. Help us find bits of joy in the midst of despair and trust you with the outcome.
Amen.

DAY 66: WARNING

Happy is the man who finds wisdom, and the man who gains understanding; for her proceeds are better than the profits of silver, and her gain than fine gold.
~ Proverbs 3:13–14 NKJV

As the rays of the sun broke through the darkness, I opened my garage door and pushed my sizable garbage can to the street.

To my left, upright trash containers and recycling bins lined the street. But to the right, I saw a vastly different picture. Five huge waste receptacles had been tossed onto sidewalks and lawns like a mini-tornado hit. Scattered refuse and slit trash bags littered sidewalks and spilled over onto the street with a long trail of debris.

On closer inspection, I saw a peanut butter jar and the remains of several meals. Down the street from those five homes, the green waste containers stood like sentinels guarding the neighborhood.

Since our development shares land with a preservation area, I frequently see eagles, turkeys, deer, ducks, coyotes, raccoons, and bears. Most of them stay in the conservation zones, but not always.

The devastation from the overturned giant-sized waste containers looked like the handiwork of a hungry bear or two. They could easily knock over the cans and rip open bags with their long claws, then rummage through the garbage for tasty bits of food. As their habitat decreased with more and more trees destroyed, they were now scavenging leftovers from human meals.

Our weekly newsletter reminds residents to put garbage out in the morning to prevent bears from venturing onto our streets and into the trash at night. However, not everyone obeys the warning. For years nothing happened, so people continued to ignore the danger. One day that changed. Fortunately, no one was hurt, there was no permanent damage, and the messes were cleaned up.

Warnings crowd our lives. Dear Lord, help us know what to heed and what to ignore.

Father, give us wisdom as we hear warnings all around us.
Give us instructions on which ones to follow.
Amen.

DAY 67: A NEW YEAR

*Do not conform to the pattern of this world, but be transformed by
the renewing of your mind. Then you will be able to test and
approve what God's will is—his good, pleasing and perfect will.*
~Romans 12:2

My mind traveled way back to the previous century. As a young girl, I blissfully enjoyed my childhood in the 1950s. During the 1960s in college, I read the book *1984* about an unimaginable and government-controlling life far in the future—and I couldn't imagine what life would look like in the 1980s.

Decades have passed since then. Horrible predictions were made for the turn of the century, but nothing spectacular happened. When I looked back at the turn of the century ushering us into Y2K, I remembered good times and hard ones. Even this past year produced some unfavorable flashbacks.

But as I faced a new year, I looked forward to better times despite the chaos and confusion in the world. Instead of my plans for the future, I prayed to know God's plans for me. I prayed for him to lead me to people who need love and encouragement. Perhaps they'd need a listening ear, a hug, or to know about Jesus. As a widow, I have learned to make plans but to be flexible when God nudges me in a different direction or to a specific situation.

During my devotional time on New Year's Day, I began a list of people who came to mind. Some faced difficult situations. Others joined my list but I didn't know why yet. I would contact each one in some way.

While I enjoy helping people, I know I also need a time of rest. During this year, I plan to work on God's timetable more than mine. Retreat and rest when I need it. I also plan on making positive changes that truly transform my mind and life.

If you don't know Jesus and want true transformation and peace, what better time to meet him than now?

> *Holy Father, thank you for another year. Keep us from being conformed to the world but transform us by the renewing of our minds.*
> *Amen.*

DAY 68: EMPTY SHELVES AND LIVES

No, in all these things we are more than conquerors through him who loved us. For I am convinced that neither death nor life, neither angels nor demons, neither the present nor the future, nor any powers, neither height nor depth, nor anything else in all creation, will be able to separate us from the love of God that is in Christ Jesus our Lord.
~ Romans 8:37–39

Bare shelves stared back at me as I sat on my couch. For weeks, my collection of nativity sets from across the globe filled every shelf of my entertainment center. Each one held a special place in my heart and brought unique memories.

My parents' ceramic one brought memories of being at their home. A few were homemade ones from family members. They all made me smile and remember Jesus's birth. After Christmas, I kept them out for a couple of weeks even though all other Christmas decorations were put away.

Every nativity portrayed Jesus in a different way. They were made of olive wood, ceramic, stone, pottery, and glass.

The artists created a distinct image of baby Jesus to fit the set they made.

At the start of February, I carefully wrapped the pieces and stored them for next year, but I didn't fill the shelves right away. A large nativity from Peru, featuring a tall church, remained as a permanent decoration. On the top shelf was an olive wood sculpture from Israel of Mary, Joseph, and baby Jesus. Each treasure reminded me of our Savior.

For a couple of days, I stared at the void the absent nativities left in my home. It reminded me of how my life would be without Jesus.

Weeks later, I returned wooden animal carvings from our trips around the world to the shelves. I lovingly added two painted ostrich eggs from Africa. One showed the Last Supper and the other was of African animals.

Along with souvenirs of our travels, I added some wooden plaques inscribed with "Blessed," "Trust in the Lord" (Proverbs 3:5), "Don't Worry About Anything But Pray About Everything" (Philippians 4:6), and "Do Not Let Your Heart Be Troubled" (John 14:1).

In our broken world, many people try to fill the void in their lives with money, fame, relationships, drugs, alcohol, entertainment, or employment, but they still remain empty and lost. God gave us the perfect solution. Knowing Jesus fills that emptiness.

Heavenly Father, thank you for loving us in all circumstances.
Nothing can separate us from the love of Jesus
that can fill our void.
Amen.

DAY 69: FLICKERING FLAMES

Nor do they light a lamp and put it under a basket,
but on a lampstand, and it gives light
to all who are in the house.
Let your light so shine before men, that they may see
your good works and glorify your Father in heaven.
~ Matthew 5:15–16 NKJV

Chilly temperatures kept me inside for my devotional time. Before dawn, one lamp illuminated my dark living room. I settled down on my couch with my Bible, devotional books, and journals.

The two candles I had lit the previous evening caught my attention. Normally, I burned them only at night, but another thought entered my mind. *Why not light them in the darkness of morning too?*

One match lit both—a short cranberry candle and a taller white one. I stared at the fascinating pointed flames that rose above the wax. They swirled in circles even though I felt no breeze. They danced and then stopped to rest. Flames stretched upward in a thinner fire, then downward and more compressed. An unseen draft altered their shapes and movement, but they continued to burn and brighten my living room.

Jesus commanded his followers to be lights in the world. We have the same directives in our dark world. Our present days certainly need light and hope. We should shine even in difficult circumstances. Our flames can dance, lengthen, and shorten, but should not go out.

Knowing Jesus keeps our lights burning brightly even when darkness and despair attempt to snuff us out. When we become weary and discouraged, the Holy Spirit recharges us. God's Word refreshes us. Jesus's light ignites us and keeps us burning.

Father, show us how to be lights in the world and keep us burning
even when we are discouraged and in despair.
Help us show your love to a hurting world.
Amen.

DAY 70: PEELING SHOES

*When pride comes, then comes disgrace,
but with humility comes wisdom.
~ Proverbs 11:2*

Oh no. How could I have not noticed?

After months of not seeing my friend, we had met for lunch at a small Cuban restaurant. For three hours we talked and caught up on our lives during isolation. She dropped me off at home, and when I took off my shoes, I almost fainted with embarrassment.

That morning, I dressed carefully in black pants and a bright blue sweater. I put on a special necklace and dabbed on a touch of makeup. Since it was cool, I went to the garage, where I found a pair of closed-toed black shoes that I rarely wear in warm, sunny Florida. It had been over a year since I wore the flats, but they fit comfortably when I quickly slipped them on. I had then hurried to my friend's waiting car.

In my haste to leave, I never looked down at my shoes. After months in an extremely hot garage, the fake leather had peeled off. Not one tiny spot remained. Both shoes peeled like they had a bad case of sunburn.

At first, I was mortified that my friend and other customers in the restaurant had seen my damaged footwear. Then as I examined the pathetic shoes more closely, I started laughing. The flawed shoes provided the perfect idea for a story.

How often have I fixed myself up to look good on the outside but ignored my bad attitude? Perhaps I judged someone who did something I didn't like. Maybe they didn't look right for church. If someone noticed my defective loafers, they might have judged me too.

My ruined footwear didn't keep me from enjoying lunch with my friend. However, if we jump to conclusions, the result can affect our peace, relationships, and Christian witness.

Lord, help us not jump to conclusions and judge others. Thank you for a sense of humor that helps me laugh at myself, and for your gift of humility that brings wisdom.
Amen.

DAY 71: OUT-OF-SEASON BUTTERFLIES

Sing to Him, sing psalms to Him;
Talk of all His wondrous works!
Glory in His holy name;
Let the hearts of those rejoice who seek the LORD!
Seek the LORD and His strength; Seek His face evermore!
Remember His marvelous works which He has done,
His wonders, and the judgments of His mouth,
~ Psalm 105:2–5 NKJV

My sluggish body longed for more sleep, but my active mind disagreed. Hours before dawn, I padded to my kitchen for a cup of tea.

Normally, I spend my devotional time outside, but cold weather and darkness had recently kept me in the house. Cool but not cold air greeted me when I opened the door. *Should I stay in or go outside?*

The outdoors won. With my tea and books, I ventured onto the shadowy patio. A solitary lamp lit my way and illuminated pages as I read the Bible and devotional books. There wasn't enough light to see outside.

Although I couldn't distinguish anything beyond the screen, I knew I wasn't alone. Noisy crows cawed to one another. Cars hummed down the interstate. Leaves rustled close by.

Could it be squirrels, raccoons, deer, or a bear? I had seen all of them around the lake. I stared into the darkness for a moment and then continued reading. Only a screen separated me from whatever lurked in my yard.

Little by little, dim outlines of ducks, flowers, and trees appeared. Semidarkness revealed a lake that wiggled with tiny waves. A hint of color tinged the sky and quickly dissolved.

After refilling my teacup, I glanced into the mostly dark butterfly cage by my chair. Every morning I checked to see if any monarchs had emerged. In winter, they usually migrate to warmer areas, but five late-season chrysalises developed in my cage. As I started to move away, I noticed a change.

Two butterflies, with wings folded, hung like statues from the mesh top. *How long have they been there?*

Perhaps they had waited all night but seemed content and not ready to be released. In the twilight, I couldn't see their vibrant colors but knew I would later observe the delicate creatures more fully.

The beautiful, out-of-season monarchs reminded me we should search for other miracles of hope and peace in our unsettled world.

> *Jehovah, as we face trials in a turbulent world, help us*
> *seek you and your miracles, even small ones, that*
> *remind us of your love, care, and peace.*
> *Amen.*

DAY 72: STARKNESS OF A WINTER DAY

*Grace to you
and peace from
God our Father and
the Lord Jesus Christ.
~ Ephesians 1:2 NKJV*

Like a black curtain, darkness enclosed my patio. My warm robe hugged me as I snuggled into my patio chair and began reading and praying.

After a while, the ebony drape lifted and revealed a thin, gray curtain. The filmy fog obscured nearby trees and concealed the lake and forest. A hidden cardinal broke the silence by chirping insistently. But no other bird answered.

Minutes later, a shadowy bird perched alone and silent on a naked limb high in one of the trees along the shore.

Amid the hazy dawn, I studied the cypress trees. Held securely by strong roots, each wide trunk tapered to a point at the top. Five stood like soldiers at attention. But a hurricane had caused one to lean slightly to the right and another to the left.

Sturdy limbs protruded from the trunks, and most angled upward. However, a few pointed to the ground. Several zigzagged like they couldn't decide which direction to grow.

Stripped, jumbled branches burst from limbs haphazardly and grew interwoven with those of neighboring trees. It was impossible to solve the puzzle of intertwining boughs.

The unique picture of light and dark held my attention. The starkness of a winter morning fog evoked a sense of peace. A silent, solitary bird intrigued me.

A gentle peacefulness settled over the lake and my thoughts. It gave me time to relax and escape the turmoil of the outside world. God's Word came alive again and spoke to my heart with promises, instructions, and commands.

Fog remained after dawn to shield me a little longer as I prepared to leave my sanctuary and enter the uncertain but often exciting world.

Father, thank you for the times of waiting, learning, and relaxing.
Show us hope and peace in your creation.
Amen.

DAY 73: A NOSTALGIC PINWHEEL

Truly he is my rock and my salvation;
he is my fortress, I will never be shaken.
~ Psalm 62:2

On a whim, I placed a brightly colored Dollar Tree pinwheel in my basket on a recent shopping trip. I certainly didn't need it, but the plastic toy reminded me of my childhood.

Occasionally, my parents had bought them for my brother and me. We blew hard to make them spin. Often, we waved our arms back and forth to create a breeze to make the wheel go round and round. However, the best times were when we held the playthings high and the wind spun and whirled the gadget like the windmill next to our house. In a simpler time, a cheap toy gave two young children hours of fun.

When I got home from the store, I stuck the multicolored pinwheel in the ground by my patio. The gaudy decoration stood out among my lovely flowers, but I smiled at the memories it evoked.

Most days the pinwheel waited patiently for a breeze. Once in a while, it revolved a couple of rounds and stopped. Despite the lack of wind, the toy continued to shine brightly in my yard.

But when strong gusts blew across the lake, the miniature windmill spun furiously. I wondered if the inexpensive toy would fly apart. It didn't. In fact, the pinwheel looked the same even though it had been through intense heat, near-freezing temperatures, and summer storms.

After careful examination, I noticed the wooden dowel that held the pieces together. As long as the linchpin stayed tight and in place, the pinwheel could withstand the ravages of the weather.

That little toy reminded me of my life. Sometimes I wait impatiently for something to happen. Then periods of activity come. I enjoy productive times until suddenly everything stops abruptly. Storms hit and I spin almost out of control. Then peace returns for a while.

Like my little pinwheel, when we have a strong anchor, we can withstand the waiting, interruptions, and trials. God is the anchor that securely holds us together.

Loving Father, you give special gifts to your children in their early years and in golden ones. In all circumstances, you are our rock when life can seem out of control. Thank you.
Amen.

DAY 74: NEGLECTED PLANTS

If some fail to do what God requires, it's as if they forget the word as soon as they hear it. One minute they look in the mirror, and the next they forget who they are and what they look like. However, it is possible to open your eyes and take in the beautiful, perfect truth found in God's law of liberty and live by it. *If you pursue that path and actually do what God has commanded, then you will avoid* the many distractions that lead *to an amnesia of all true things and you will be blessed.*
~ James 1:23–25 VOICE

Frost covered my neighbor's roof like a layer of new snow. The scene was out of place in subtropical Florida, but the sun melted it quickly without a trace.

For weeks our weather reports shifted from cold to warm and cool to hot. On nippy nights, I carefully wrapped protective cloth around my collection of orchids, spider plants, and herbs on my patio. When I received a frost alert, I also covered outside blooming plants like poinsettias and mums.

Cover and then uncover. A few days later, it was time to cover again.

When it warmed up, I neglected to care for my delicate plants. Other activities and concerns took my attention. One morning, a brisk forty-five-degree temperature greeted me as I opened the patio door.

I cringed, looking at my uncovered orchids. I saw no immediate damage but wondered if they would still flourish and bloom since the temps were way below the suggested environment for orchids. For weeks, I carefully tended them. Then life got busy and I disregarded them again.

In the same way, it is easy to write prayer requests in a journal and list church leaders, government authorities, family members, and friends who need prayer. For a while, each person is prayed for faithfully. Then distractions come. Prayers decrease and sometimes even stop.

At the beginning of the year, a resolution might be made to read the Bible daily and finish in a year. For me, January goes well. February is pretty good, but then as the year progresses, the Bible reading doesn't. More pressing things take over.

Hopefully, my neglected plants will survive with little injury. Perhaps loving care will restore their vibrancy.

Not only do my plants need nurturing, but so do I. When I read my Bible daily, meditate on what I read, and pray, my life is refreshed and nourished. Especially during trying times, I find it essential to stay connected to Jesus.

Jehovah, I know you give us strength to face trials and difficulties.
Help us stay connected to you and not get distracted.
Amen.

DAY 75: FROM FOG TO SUNSHINE

*You are the lamp who lights my way; the Eternal, my God, lights
up my darkness.
With Your help, I can conquer an army;
I can leap over walls with a helping hand from You.
Everything God does is perfect;
the promise of the Eternal rings true;
He stands as a shield for all who hide in Him.
~ Psalm 18:28–30 VOICE*

A cool breeze swept across the obscured lake. While on the patio, I shivered under my blanket. My tea grew cold quickly. Frosty air invigorated me as I wrote in my gratitude journal and added more names to my prayer journal.

During my devotional time, dim light revealed a lake with mysterious trees surrounding it. Pines swayed, and daisies danced in the wind. Leaves rustled both near me and across the water. The sun crept behind the forest and shone like a beacon through the trees and onto the rippling lake. The cloak of darkness opened to an azure sky.

Although the view from my patio had not changed from the day before, the picture appeared quite different. Instead of fog blurring the landscape, sunlight made everything brighter. Green grass sparkled from the night's shower. Strong winds swept away all traces of dreariness. A glowing sun spread rays in all directions. Large birds soared with the strong currents.

An overnight storm pushed away yesterday's gloom. Sunshine replaced fog and brought a dazzling, new day. Because of the previous day's dreariness, the sunshine seemed even more brilliant and beautiful to me.

Life is a series of storms and sunshine with ups and downs. But after we face a period of darkness, the emerging light gleams even brighter.

Loving Father, thank you for lighting our way in the storms and providing a shield to protect us.
Amen.

DAY 76: STANDING STRONG IN THE STORMS

The LORD is my strength and my shield;
my heart trusts in him, and he helps me.
My heart leaps for joy, and with my song I praise him.
~ Psalm 28:7

A predicted cold front brought leaden, menacing clouds racing across the sky. Darkness threatened long before dusk. Blustery winds raged.

When I stepped onto my porch to move furniture closer to the house, I noticed a blue heron standing near the shoreline, surveying the lake. The impending weather forced me inside, but he remained steadfast by the water.

As the sky darkened, I noticed the blue heron knee deep in water in front of my house. His profile was that of a strong, stoic solider. He stood erect with his long bill pointed toward the approaching storm. Trees reeled around him. Gusts whipped limbs and ruffled his feathers. Nevertheless, he stood like a statue as if defying the gales to knock him over.

He didn't cower or hide. Not a bellow or whimper came from his beak. He remained calm in the midst of the storm.

While I watched the majestic bird, I thought of the example he displayed of how to face difficulties and storms. Stand firm. Face it. Don't let it knock you down. The lone bird's example convicted me that I too can weather the storms of life and isolation, whether they are from a virus, a divorce, grief, illness, incarceration, or another trial.

Thankfully, Jesus offers hope, love, and encouragement to those who know him. He helps us face the storms, stand strong, and defeat the winds of despair. When we encounter storms, we don't have to do it alone.

Heavenly Father, as we go through our storms and think there is no end, we can trust you to give us strength and be our shield. Thank you for loving us when the world is beating us up.
Amen.

DAY 77: A BRIGHT SPOT IN THE GLOOM

When Jesus spoke again to the people, he said,
"I am the light of the world. Whoever follows me will never walk in
darkness, but will have the light of life."
~ John 8:12

Heavy clouds cast a feeling of melancholy around the lake. They blocked sunlight, subdued colorful flowers, and darkened the water.

Only a few melodies drifted to my patio as most birds remained quiet in the dismal morning. None roamed along the shoreline or swam in the lake.

But despite the dreariness, a trio of bees gathered within my orange and white flowers. Blooms dipped as tiny creatures clung to bell-shaped flowers. After days of rain and little sunshine, I certainly welcomed some cheerfulness.

When I stared at the bleak scene before me, a dazzling red figure darted from my oak tree to a nearby cypress. The scarlet cardinal provided a bright spot in the gloom. His color made me smile and reminded me that despite feelings of despair, there are other bright spots in the world.

News of sicknesses, floods, wildfires, earthquakes, rioting, and constant discord has brought desperation and anxiety to us as people and a nation. It is easy to fall into a pit of hopelessness if we put our trust in things of the world.

However, knowing and trusting Jesus gives us assurance, peace, and strength for our present troubles and the unknown future. Instead of joining in the misery of worry and fearfulness of life, I look for bright spots in a dismal world.

As Christians, we can be beacons of hope and encouragement to those who are struggling.

Heavenly Father, thank you for being a light in the world. Show us how we can be light to others who only see darkness.
Amen.

DAY 78: UNAPPRECIATED THUMBS

So support one another. Keep building each other up as you have been doing. Brothers and sisters, we ask you to show appreciation to those who are working hard among you and those who are your leaders as they guide and instruct you in the Lord—they are priceless. When you think about them, let it be with great love in your heart because of all the work they have done. Let peace live and reign among you.
~ 1 Thessalonians 5:11–13 VOICE

Throbbing pain interrupted my sleep. During the day, it curtailed my normal routine.

Each day, my thumb grew larger and redder. Every touch caused more torment. Holding a toothbrush, grasping the steering wheel, or writing with a pen brought suffering. When I utilized my right hand for anything, the pain increased. Compared to my fingers, the swollen thumb looked like a short, chubby finger banished and stuck on the side of my hand.

Whenever I used my left hand, chores took me forever or I couldn't do them at all. Unloading the dishwasher took about three times as long as normal. I couldn't latch the clasp on a necklace without my right thumb, so I gave up.

As I endured discomfort for several days, I marveled at how pain in such a small part of my body affected my life. It consumed me and restricted all my daily activities. I never appreciated the importance and need for a thumb until mine was incapacitated. None of my other fingers could take its place.

The agony and reduced use of my thumb humbled me. I thought of people with no thumbs or hands. Those who endured intense suffering every day. My minor inconvenience didn't compare to their trials.

A trip to the doctor brought a diagnosis and antibiotics for an infection. I no longer winced each time I touched my thumb and was thankful the red, swollen digit started to look healthy again. No longer would I ignore the often-unnoticed thumb but value every task it handles.

Like my unappreciated thumb, first responders and health care workers who faithfully served during the pandemic have not always been recognized as they performed their work in extremely difficult and often dangerous situations. However, they, like my now-healthy thumb, continue to be vital in helping us get through an unprecedented time.

Loving Father, show us how to appreciate and encourage people in the background who keep things going for us.
Also, thank you for designing our bodies with perfect but sometimes unappreciated parts.
Amen.

DAY 79: ANOTHER DAY OF BLEAKNESS?

He says,
"Be still and know that I am God;
I will be exalted among the nations,
I will be exalted in the earth."
~ Psalm 46:10

Day after day, dreariness engulfed the sun. Rain and clouds dominated. The weather in Florida, "The Sunshine State," didn't live up to its appealing name. To make matters worse, weather reports announced an approaching hurricane. Meteorologists continuously predicted torrential rains, damaging winds, and destructive storms.

The worst of the hurricane didn't hit my part of the state but caused heavy rain and gales. Throughout that time, God prodded me to be thankful despite the storms. I needed to look for flickers of light in the gloom.

Lakes returned to normal levels after the drought ended. Rain prevented wildfires and refreshed the parched earth.

Flowers brightened. Grass greened up. Ducks splashed in the rain.

Bees continued to visit droopy flowers. A mama cardinal plucked worms from the soggy ground while papa stood watch from a low branch.

Cypress limbs, heavy with water, swayed in the breezes. A songbird's tune drifted through the rain. A doe and her two fawns romped on the shore across the lake.

When I looked for God in the midst of the dismal weather, a sense of tranquility wrapped me like an exquisite shawl laced with rest and peace.

God often slows us down so we can relax, learn, and prepare for what lies ahead. Each day, be thankful. Listen for his still, small voice and look for blessings in the trials.

Heavenly Father, it is easy to complain about life's difficult circumstances. Help us be still and look for you in each situation.
Amen.

DAY 80: A STUBBORN ATTITUDE

I will instruct you and teach you in the way you should go;
I will counsel you with my loving eye on you.
~ Psalm 32:8

The two-year-old girl whom my granddaughter, Ashlyn, was babysitting, motioned for a banana. But after a couple of bites, she noticed the freshly baked cookies on the counter. Suddenly, her fruit lost its appeal and she asked for a cookie.

"You can have a cookie when you finish your banana," Ashlyn responded.

As fast as tiny legs could take her across the kitchen, the little one threw her banana, peel and all, into the trash. Then she looked at Ashlyn with pleading eyes and said, "Cookie?"

In the little one's mind, the unacceptable situation had been taken care of: get rid of the banana and get the cookie.

Watching the interaction, I intervened. "She can't get away with that," I said. "You have to be firm."

Ashlyn agreed as she pulled the fruit from the garbage. It had not touched anything unpleasant because of the peel, so we decided it would be safe to eat.

The determined toddler ignored the banana and continued asking for a cookie.

Ashlyn repeated, "You can have a cookie when you finish your banana."

Back and forth went the same conversation. Finally, there was a compromise. If she ate two bites of the remaining banana, she would get a cookie. She ate two bites and then enjoyed the homemade treat.

As we laughed about her stubbornness, I thought about how I have done the same thing when God leads me on a certain path. I want to ignore his instructions and get my own way, informing him of what I want. He tells me what I must do first. Back and forth we go. Sometimes I continue to plead my case and then follow my own desires, which often brings painful consequences. However, when I listen and follow his plans, the results are so much better than mine.

If we stopped being so stubborn, prayed, and listened to God, we could avoid some of our less-than-desirable outcomes.

Jehovah-Nissi, you see what lies ahead and where the victory will be. Help us learn to listen and follow your plans and not our own.
Amen.

DAY 81: ME, SELFISH?

Let your conversation be always full of grace, seasoned with salt, so that you may know how to answer everyone.
~ *Colossians 4:6*

A breakfast of scrambled eggs, bacon, sausage, and fried potatoes awaited church volunteers who ate before their assigned serving times. My friend and I picked up our plates and waited until the disheveled man in front of us finished heaping food on his plate. He grabbed a ketchup bottle and squeezed a large red blob onto his food.

A week earlier, Mike and I had decided we needed ketchup, so we were glad someone had brought a bottle of it. When the man started toward the door with the condiment in his hand, I asked, "Is there any more ketchup?"

His answer shocked me. Without even a glance, he stated, "I bought it." Then he left with the bottle in hand.

Stunned, we shook our heads. I couldn't even think of a response, I was so dumbfounded by his selfishness.

For years, the rumpled man has appeared soon after breakfast was set out. He doesn't volunteer and rarely talks to anyone. I have never seen him attend a service, but he loves the food.

When I have tried to engage him in conversation, he ignores me or answers me with one word. I assumed he was homeless but found out he isn't and does have a job.

All week the scenario played in my mind. *Should someone tell him he is selfish? Should we let him continue to be that way? Which would be most helpful?*

As I pondered his deplorable behavior, God nudged me about my own attitudes. Thoughts started pouring in. *Am I selfish about my resources and time? Is my time more valuable to me than comforting someone who is grieving? Do I ignore a person who grates on my nerves because I don't want to waste my time? Do I grab ahold of what God has given me and hold onto it tightly as well?*

My behavior might not be as blatant as that of the man at church, but guilt from my selfishness remained. Perhaps our breakfast is the best meal of his week. Maybe he has trouble relating to people and doesn't know what to say. Hopefully, being at church and seeing Christians who let him have a meal might lead him to Jesus.

Alan used to say, "We never know what others are going through." In hindsight, I'm glad I didn't say anything to him. The last thing I would want is to be a barrier to someone else accepting and loving Jesus.

God used the man's inconsiderate behavior to make me take a closer look at myself.

Lord, you use all kinds of situations to teach us how we should be living. Each day, show me how to be more like you.
Amen.

DAY 82: CLOAKED WITH PEACE

*You will keep in perfect peace
those whose minds are steadfast,
because they trust in you.
~ Isaiah 26:3*

Rumbles of thunder broke the morning's silence. Clouds darkened the sky and blocked the sun. Out-of-sight crows screeched. Songbirds remained silent. Bees visited flowers, but no other wildlife appeared.

Thunder grew louder and more frequent. The wind rustled trees on the far shore and then swept closer. A sheet of rain followed close behind. First, it raced over the lake and then hit the shore and my yard.

Tall cypress trees shook heavy limbs as though trying to remove the blasts of water. The smaller oak tree quivered when washed by the rain. Flower leaves jiggled with each drop. Droplets coated my screen. Mist and cooler air caressed my arms.

Eventually, the wind ceased and a soft rain replaced the torrents. Gentle, long waves traveled from shore to shore.

Like a giant watering can, rain refreshed grass, flowers, and trees. The lake level rose. Much-needed moisture brought renewal. God knows his creation requires sunshine and rain to flourish. In wonder, I watched the shower and marveled at his provision.

When I spend time with God each morning, watching nature intently reminds me that he provides for all his creation, from tiny bees to tall cypress trees to—especially—his people.

Just as the rain comes and refreshes creation, God's love showers us with blessings, refreshes us, and cloaks us with his peace.

Jehovah-Shalom, the provision you give to your creation includes us. Thank you for the comfort, love, and peace you so generously provide.
Amen.

DAY 83: SHATTERED PIECES

*Do not be anxious about anything, but in every situation, by
prayer and petition, with thanksgiving,
present your requests to God.
And the peace of God, which transcends all understanding, will
guard your hearts and your minds in Christ Jesus.
~ Philippians 4:6–7*

Crash!

From my office, I hurried to the kitchen to see what caused the sound of breaking glass. Nothing was out of place. Then I walked into the living room. A large African basket had fallen from its spot at the top of the entertainment center, but it certainly wouldn't make the loud racket.

As I moved closer to the basket, sharp slivers jabbed my feet. I noticed white fragments strewn across the wood floor and rug.

While I gathered the shards, I realized what had caused the mishap. The basket hit a plaque that stood on a lower shelf before it plummeted to the floor. A corner of it broke off into pieces of all sizes. The circular basket stood upright at the back of the top shelf but must have slowly slipped and hit the decoration on its way to the floor.

The broken memento wasn't as expensive or irreplaceable as most of the other treasures on my shelves. However, the Scripture written on it was one of my favorites.

For a second, I thought of throwing the damaged plaque away, but I changed my mind. As I glued shattered fragments back together, gaps remained but I kept the mended memento to remind me of my own brokenness.

The verse from Philippians gave me comfort when I was stressed: "Be anxious for nothing."

When our splintered lives cause anxiety, Jesus offers peace and contentment as he creates something beautiful from the wreckage.

Father, thank you for gluing our shattered lives together and creating something magnificent.
Amen.

DAY 84: THE MASSIVE SPIDER WEB

Plans fall apart without proper *advice;*
but with the right guidance,
they come together nicely.
~ Proverbs 15:22 VOICE

Sunlight struck my face as the sun rose above the trees. As I squinted and looked toward the lake, I noticed a glistening masterpiece suspended from my oak tree. For several minutes I gazed at it in awe.

As I looked through my binoculars, the intricacies of the delicate web came into focus. A silver thread attached the top of the web to a high branch about twenty feet from the ground. Five or six strands hung from the bottom, but their ends eluded me. The little critter must have had to drop ten or fifteen feet from the top of the tree to form the first strand of the web.

I stared intently at the silky creation. The giant web contained thick fibers radiating from the center like spokes on a wheel. More threads wove round and round between them in an extraordinary, lacy design.

After all that work, something had hit or flew through the web and made two sizable holes The captivating creation brought so many questions to my mind. *How could a little spider construct a web so high? After working so diligently to develop it, what happened to the spider? What caused the large holes? Did the spider receive any food from the web? Was it eaten by whatever made the hole?* I will never get answers to my questions, but the whole interaction made me ponder.

During my extended time at home, I spent more time in my garden retreat enjoying the magnificence of nature around me. For months, I saw more spider webs glisten in the grass, on small bushes, and in trees than ever before. However, none had been as massive or as high as the latest one.

We, like the spider, perform tedious, demanding work to accomplish goals in our complex lives. We labor to accomplish our plan. Then losses, disappointments, illnesses, divorce, and other tragedies cause holes to form in our life plans.

But if we have a firm anchor in Jesus, He will hold us securely even when our lives seem to be falling apart.

Loving Father, what an amazing world you have made.
Thank you for everything from spider webs to our
intricate lives. You are our security in trying times.
Amen.

DAY 85: NOT COVID!

I will lie down and sleep, for you alone,
*L*ORD*, make me dwell in safety.*
~ Psalm 4:8

For over a year, COVID attacked the world, with everyone suffering directly or indirectly due to the virus. Isolation and shutdowns affected everyone. But one day my life changed dramatically with coughing, fatigue, chills, congestion, nausea, and body aches.

At first, I thought I had a bad cold and then possibly the flu. My doctor prescribed medications and told me to get a COVID test, but I didn't think I had it. After all, I had gotten vaccinated and took every precaution to be safe.

When my results came back, I stared at the computer screen. I didn't believe the bright red letters at the top. POSITIVE. No longer could I ignore the symptoms or pretend the pandemic was far from me. I had the dreaded disease.

After staying on the couch for three or four days, I hoped to quickly feel good again. That didn't happen for several more days.

Gradually, I learned to take pleasure in sights and sounds around me. From my patio, the beauty of my lake entertained me for hours. Sunlight danced on the waves. Insects hummed as they swerved around my flowers. A variety of birds swooped over the lake, dipped into the water, and walked along the shore. Their delightful tunes and calls filled the air.

Yellow buttercup blooms smiled at me. Miniature white and orange trumpet-shaped flowers attracted bees. A lengthy spider web swayed like a clothesline between two trees. The beauty of nature captivated me.

Fatigue limited my activities during my isolation, but even on my couch, I could text and send emails, although coughing limited my phone calls.

At the beginning of my sickness, reading and writing took too much strength. Later, after much rest, I was able to read again. I pored over a host of books. Hour after hour, classic shows made me laugh. Documentaries increased my knowledge on a variety of topics. My couch time wasn't totally wasted.

While in solitude, I increased my Bible reading and praying. Television shows taught me more about the Bible and Israel.

During quarantine, I learned to appreciate and embrace the quietness of my home. Thankfully, my relatively mild symptoms didn't compare to what some people endured.

Our afflictions can certainly intensify thankfulness for energy and good health.

Father, thank you for holding us when we are sick and
for giving us peace as we rest.
Amen.

DAY 86: DON'T TAKE AWAY BLESSINGS

For I testify that they gave as much as they were able, and even beyond their ability. Entirely on their own, they urgently pleaded with us for the privilege of sharing in this service to the Lord's people.
~ *2 Corinthians 8:3–4*

Although I couldn't venture out of my home for a few weeks, many of my friends came to me. They blessed me with chicken soup and ginger ale when I didn't feel like eating. After I regained my appetite, fruit, yogurt, apples, and oranges appeared at my doorstep. Then complete, delicious meals arrived. Books showed up to keep me occupied.

My phone stayed busy with text messages, emails, and calls. Five bouquets of flowers turned up to make me smile. Each item filled me with gratitude and soothed my weary soul.

During that time, our sermon series at church, "Blessed," reminded me how God used my friends to reach out and follow Jesus's instruction to love one another. Because I enjoy helping others, it has always been really hard to accept assistance. But when COVID kept me down, I had no choice but to receive, since I was alone.

Day after day, friends provided care, meals, and notes of encouragement. I marveled at God's provisions and hadn't expected such an outpouring of love and compassion. He multiplied my tiny acts of kindness into huge blessings.

When I comfort and assist someone, I am thankful for the opportunity. During my isolation, I had few occasions to do it. However, when I saw smiles and a continual stream of loving gifts, I realized that by serving me, my friends were being blessed too.

Trying to be too self-sufficient is a form of selfishness. When we refuse kindnesses and offers of help, we take away another person's blessing.

No one wants to be selfish.

Father, show us how to bless others and also how to graciously accept help.
Amen.

DAY 87: THE YELLOW MUMS

God has not given us a spirit of fear,
but of power and love and a sound mind.
~ 2 Timothy 1:7 NKJV

Last summer, yellow mums formed a border in front of my shrubs. Their vibrant color even showed up from down the street. A few of the plants remained from the previous summer, but I purchased more to add to the display. However, I didn't plant them when I got home. Then the next day I discovered that I had COVID.

For days I shuffled past them on my journey to the mailbox and wondered when I would ever have the strength to dig holes for them. A few times I watered the droopy plants, which for me was a major accomplishment. Finally, I had enough energy to get them into the ground, right before they died.

After my isolation ended, I made more trips to the store to purchase additional flowers. But the cheerful mums always warmed my heart and energized my still-fatigued body. For weeks, they gave brightness to my yard and the neighborhood.

Eventually, the yellow buds turned brown. The once-gorgeous plants turned to ugly, brown clumps. I wondered if I should just dig them up.

But within a few weeks, tiny green leaves appeared at the bottom of the brown lumps. After that, tiny yellow blooms joined the foliage.

Would the new growth overtake the ugliness? When I grew tired of the dried, dead leaves, I used my lawn shears to cut some of them off. Unsightly stubs that were once healthy stems remained, but I ignored them for a few days.

When I started to feel better and couldn't stand it any longer, I sat on the ground by the first flower and used small clippers to remove every dead stem from the new growth. I scooted down the row and pruned every plant. The job took much longer than when I used the big shears, but the result amazed me.

My flowers looked new and healthy. Their color lifted my spirits and reminded me that we often have to be pruned too. When we prune unhealthy habits, fear, worry, and unforgiveness from our lives, we can become healthier and more vibrant too.

Lord, help us get rid of those things that prevent us from living the life you desire for us.
Amen.

DAY 88: UNCLEAN—STAY AWAY!

*"Peace I leave with you; my peace I give you.
I do not give to you as the world gives.
Do not let your hearts be troubled and do not be afraid."*
~ John 14:27

"Unclean! Stay away!"

In biblical times, those with leprosy had to yell out if anyone came near them. Everyone considered lepers to be unclean, so they lived away from family and friends, isolated and rejected by society.

In one episode of *The Chosen*, a TV series about Jesus, a leper went to Jesus to be healed. The disciples warned Jesus to stay away from the sick man, but our Lord ignored them and touched the man anyway. For someone completely rejected by society, human touch would have been a miracle in itself. Jesus, through his touch, healed the diseased man.

As I watched the show, I identified with those isolated from family, friends, and even strangers. During my seclusion, I stayed inside for days. No one came into my home.

Wonderful friends brought food, medications, flowers, and books, but left them at my door. They rang the doorbell and walked away.

Only then would I open the door, after they had left, and gather their gifts so they would not be infected. Although it was necessary, being isolated made me feel like a leper.

When I started feeling better, I spoke to my friends from my doorstep as they greeted me from the end of my walkway. Just seeing a person and having a short conversation from ten feet away made me feel less lonely.

Living alone can feel like you've been abandoned, but during the pandemic, it became more intense. I didn't yell "COVID!" or "Unclean!" when friends came to my door, but I felt like an outcast for a while. After two weeks of no human touch, when arms finally encircled me, a sense of relief, revival, and blessing washed over me.

During the pandemic, millions of people were isolated and many were totally alone like I was. No hugs, smiles, or even a pat on the back. Around the world, people have been deeply affected by isolation. Hopefully, we have learned how important it is to be connected to others. As we leave our homes and venture out, we can show friendship, appreciation, and love to others.

Give hugs, hold a hand, or pat a shoulder. Share little gestures of friendship and love.

God, even in our distress and solitude, you remove fear and give us peace. You remain faithful and will never leave us.
Amen.

DAY 89: THE RETREAT IN NEW HAMPSHIRE

We are confident that God is able to orchestrate everything to work toward something good and beautiful *when we love Him and accept His invitation to live according to His plan.*
~ Romans 8:28 VOICE

Heavy, gray clouds blocked all traces of an anticipated sunrise. Rain peppered the roof of the hotel's veranda. Clouds enveloped the mountaintops and reduced them to hills.

A collection of trees filled the valley and crept toward the peaks. Tall evergreens hovered over golden, amber, and brown trees. Bare white birches stood at attention along the edge of the woods. Together they formed a picturesque but muted forest in the White Mountains of New Hampshire. I had hoped to see an infusion of brilliant colors splattered over the landscape, but days of heavy rain caused the leaves to darken and drop.

For two days rain kept me inside the grand, historic hotel with limited views of the expansive grounds. Although my experience didn't meet my expectations of vibrant, autumn colors, the cooler weather and subdued hues provided a welcome change from warm and green Florida. I marveled at the difference between this woodland creation and my lake view.

Seated on the long porch, I noticed a stream that emerged from the forest and rushed along the rocky banks. Mist slipped down the Appalachian Mountains and obscured more of the timberland. A serene peacefulness settled over me as I watched the changing view.

After my bout of COVID, the Asbury Seminary Retreat provided peace and healing for me. Speakers from the school spoke to my heart. Wonderful music soothed my soul. I enjoyed meeting interesting new friends.

I wondered who should get the books I wrote on grieving that were packed in my suitcase. My grief ministry expanded as I heard stories of loss from other participants. I gave out books to three people who had recently lost loved ones.

Although my expectations for vivid fall colors didn't materialize, the subtle beauty of the mountains and countryside supplied tranquility and a time for heartfelt contemplation.

Throughout life, plans change and hopes are dashed. Instead of lamenting over losses, we can embrace new opportunities and see what surprises God has planned.

Heavenly Father, when our plans are thwarted, you know what lies ahead and can turn it into something good.
Amen.

DAY 90: THE DIVERSE ELEVEN

He said to them, "Go into all the world and preach the gospel to all creation. Whoever believes and is baptized will be saved, but whoever does not believe will be condemned."
~ Mark 16:15–16

A flood of senior citizens descended on the conference center. They arrived from Central and North Florida, Georgia, North Carolina, and Alabama in cars, vans, and buses.

Because of isolation, the yearly event had been canceled for two years. As soon as registration opened, I signed up. Week after week, I called the camp office to add more buddies. Five years earlier, one friend joined me. The guest list increased annually. This year, I brought ten registrants.

Looking forward to our togetherness after being cooped up at home and secluded from gatherings made us almost giddy. We drove from five communities to the event.

Even though most groups consisted of members from a single church, our diverse gang of eleven came from seven congregations. With such a wide variety of denominations, our weekly services included all different styles of worship, each one filled with the love of God.

Even though we started out as a group of strangers, we began to blend together as we learned names and found mutual connections. Old friends reunited and new friendships began. At meals, common experiences and interests united us as we talked.

In a painting class we created pictures, encouraged each other, and laughed at less-than-perfect results. A seminar on ancient Jerusalem engaged the group in discussions and brought back memories of previous trips to Israel for some of us.

In the auditorium, Christian music filled the air with three hundred participants joining in to sing favorite hymns and learning some not-so-familiar songs. Two concerts entertained us but also brought out the need of earplugs for older ears.

A number of speakers spoke on a variety of thought-provoking topics. Comedy produced laughter.

For three days, our group looked out for each other as strangers became friends. Ladies from various places, both geographically and spiritually, bonded as fellow Christians. Unlike much of the world, we came together in love, joy, and acceptance with no division or condemnation.

As Christians, we are commanded to go into the world and spread the gospel. After so much isolation, the retreat provided the perfect training for Jesus's great commission.

Loving Father, bring us together as friends and not strangers.
Show us how to love and accept those who may be different
from us. Help us share the gospel with those
who don't know you.
Amen.

BONUS DAY 91: THE LOST SUITCASE

May the God of hope fill you with all joy and peace as you trust in him, so that you may overflow with hope by the power of the Holy Spirit.
~ Romans 15:13

My favorite suitcase had a broken wheel and frayed edges. I liked the size but couldn't find another one like it. Alan and I had matching sets, but he had given his away before he died. Every time I bumped along with my dilapidated one, I became more annoyed that he hadn't kept his for me.

As I put Christmas decorations into a cabinet in the garage, I noticed a larger, unblemished version of our carry-ons. When I picked it up to check the size, I was surprised by its heavy weight, so I opened it.

The luggage I thought Alan had given away had been in my garage all along. Its weightiness brought another wave of curiosity. Unzipping it unlocked more surprises.

Grief ambushed me when I looked at the contents.

It was a time capsule. Tears rolled down my face with every discovery. I picked up a boarding pass from our last mission trip to Jamaica, only three months before he passed away. Since his health had deteriorated, we knew it would be our final mission trip together.

Then came a paper from the *Sapphire Princess*—our last cruise with his brother Dave and sister-in-law Donita as we explored the Hawaiian Islands. We also met his cousin Linda and her husband, Sam, on Maui during a stop. At that time, Alan felt fine because of taking an experimental drug, so we had no idea that would be our last cruise.

Copies of our passports with younger faces. Seasickness medications. Alan's business cards from his former ministry. Shoe mittens that he always used to keep dirt off his clothes.

As I gently handled every item, my sadness grew. Memories poured down my face. But when grief ambushed, joy overtook me. Flashbacks of trips around the world to all seven continents kept me company.

In the seclusion of my garage, the Holy Spirit comforted me. My crying finally subsided. This beautiful discovery filled me with grief, wonder, and thankfulness.

A hidden suitcase, one that I thought was gone for years, materialized to provide hope. I looked forward to it accompanying me on future discoveries. Delightful memories of Alan and our adventures filled my mind and propelled me forward.

A brief time of grief for the past but joy for the future launched me toward new adventures.

As my times of isolation from illnesses, the pandemic, and loss of my beloved husband came to an end, I stood in awe of God and how he never left me. He was always there providing comfort, hope, and peace during my darkest hours.

*Heavenly Father, help us not miss the gifts you have for us.
Remind us of the happy and sad moments of life.
But also don't let us forget you are
with us in all situations.
Amen.*

AUTHOR BIO

Rebecca Carpenter was born in Frankfort, Indiana, but lived in several small communities in the farming area of the state. One town even had a stop light. She and her family left the snow for the sunshine of Central Florida while she was in college. After her long teaching career, she and her husband traveled around the world on mission and pleasure trips, where her love of photography flourished. The cover photo is from her visit to the Canadian Rockies.

She has contributed stories to ten of the *Moments* book series including *Loving Moments*, *Pandemic Moments*, and *Christmas Moments*. Focus on the Family's *Clubhouse* and *Clubhouse Jr.* magazines have featured articles she penned about her granddaughters. Rebecca has won several Word Weavers International Tapestry Awards.

Her first book of devotions, *Ambushed by Glory in My Grief,* described how God gave her comfort and encouragement after losing her parents and husband.

Rebecca's writing ideas come from the peacefulness of her lake, her delightful granddaughters, and unusual situations like broken glass piercing her foot.

ALSO BY REBECCA CARPENTER

Rebecca Carpenter also wrote, *Ambushed by Glory in My Grief,* which is available on Amazon (by scanning the QR code below) or where ever fine books are sold.

www.hopeinisolation.com

DEEP WATERS BOOKS
deepwatersbooks.com

For other fine books published
by Deep Waters Books,
visit us at www.deepwatersbooks.com
or scan the QR code below.

www.ingramcontent.com/pod-product-compliance
Lightning Source LLC
Chambersburg PA
CBHW020306010526
44107CB00001B/1